Y0-AEA-870

LETTERS FROM *Japan*

Joan Mondale

JOAN MONDALE

LETTERS FROM JAPAN

2	**Preface**	
11	**September, 1993**	*Getting the Call*
16	**October, 1993**	*Making the Rounds*
19	**February, 1994**	*Art from America in Japan*
24	**March, 1994**	*Off to Hokkaido*
27	**April, 1994**	*The Prime Minister Visits*
30	**May, 1994**	*Okinawa, the Unique Island*
34	**June, 1994**	*Mashiko, Home of Mingei Potters*
36	**June 11-15, 1994**	*The Imperial State Visit to Washington*
39	**July, 1994**	*Sumo, the National Sport*
43	**September, 1994**	*The American Festival and the Carters Come to Town*
46	**October, 1994**	*Everyone Comes to Tokyo*
51	**November, 1994**	*Hakodate*
53	**January, 1995**	*Kyushu*
57	**February, 1995**	*Digger and the Crow*
60	**March, 1995**	*Disaster in Kobe*
63	**April, 1995**	*Student Exchanges*
66	**May, 1995**	*Iwo Jima, the Sulphur Island, 50 Years Later*
70	**June, 1995**	*At Last, Our Own Home*

78	**July, 1995**	*WCCO-Radio Comes to Call, by Walter Mondale*
82	**September 2, 1995**	*Questions*
85	**October, 1995**	*Eiji Oue - Japan and Minnesota; Settling into the Residence*
88	**November, 1995**	*Izu, Peninsula of Earthquakes*
91	**December, 1995**	*Women in Japan*
94	**January, 1996**	*A Typical Week*
100	**February, 1996**	*Lunch with Their Majesties*
102	**March, 1996**	*The Cost of Living*
105	**April, 199**	*Kindling the Home Fires, A Letter from Amy Katoh*
110	**May, 1996**	*Those Ubiquitous Cherry Blossoms*
113	**June, 1996**	*The Clintons Come to Visit*
118	**July, 1996**	*Japanese Ghosts*
121	**August, 1996**	*America's Birthday, Tokyo Style*
124	**September, 1996**	*A Visit to Yokosuka and American Students in Japan*
127	**October, 1996**	*Marriage and Art in Public Places*
132	**November, 1996**	*What to See in Tokyo*
139	**December, 1996**	*Saying Good-Bye and Coming Home*
145	**March, 1997**	*From Ambassador to Grandpa*

Library of Congress
Cataloging-in-Publication Data

ISBN 0-9662220-0-8
Mondale, Joan
  Life as the wife of the U.S. Ambassador to
  Japan, 1993-1996.

Copyright © 1997
Illustrations and book design by Judy Anderson.
Text is set in Janson and Frutiger type.
Produced on chlorine free recycled paper with soy ink
by Printery Communications, Washington.

LETTERS FROM JAPAN

- Both President Clinton and Fritz enjoyed a private moment before the announcement ceremony in the Rose Garden at the White House.

Preface

It's hard to keep a secret in Washington, D.C., or in Minneapolis, Minnesota, where we were living in 1993. As soon as Bill Clinton won the presidential election in 1992, rumors started about whom he would appoint to his cabinet and as ambassadors. Fritz's name was mentioned as ambassador to the U.N., ambassador to Russia, and, finally, ambassador to Japan.

On May 13, 1993, *The Washington Post* reported that a reliable source indicated that Fritz would be appointed ambassador to Japan. Then on May 20, our Minneapolis newspaper, the *Star Tribune*, carried an article adding to the speculation. Carleton Varney, a friend who designed the tables for state dinners in the White House for President and Mrs. Jimmy Carter, called and wanted to decorate the family quarters in the residence in Tokyo. On June 4, a story about those in the White House who were supporting Fritz as the president's choice appeared in *The New York Times*. We began to wonder if the rumors were true.

At last, the phone call from the president came on Monday, June 7 at 11:30 p.m. The White House operator called our home in Minneapolis, asking for Fritz. He was in Washington, staying at the Park Hyatt Hotel. Half an hour later, Fritz called to tell me that President Clinton had asked him to serve as ambassador to

Japan, and that he had accepted the appointment. We told no one!

Two days later, on June 9, the headline "Clinton Expected to Name Mondale as Envoy to Japan" appeared in *The Washington Post*. The same day, Fritz's photograph appeared in color on the front page of both the Minneapolis and St. Paul newspapers and everyone started phoning to congratulate us. We received 41 phone calls that day alone: friends called who wanted to give farewell dinners for us, who offered to take me shopping for clothes to wear in Japan, who asked if I needed boxes for packing, and who sent arrangements of flowers. My mother called to be sure Fritz knew about our Reischauer connection. (Edwin O. Reischauer was appointed U.S. ambassador to Japan by President Kennedy and served from 1961-1966. He was my father's first cousin. His mother and my grandmother were sisters.) Our daughter

- **In 1927, uncle Karl and aunt Helen Reischauer (Edwin Reischauer's parents) invited my father, Dr. John Maxwell Adams, to teach English in the school they founded, which has become The Women's Christian College of Tokyo.**

Preface

Eleanor called to tell us that there was speculation all over the Chicago Mercantile Exchange. Pam Mondale, our daughter-in-law, reported that our grandson Louie, age 3, was telling everyone that President Clinton had asked his grandfather to hunt the Ninja Turtles! Many friends called with advice: "I understand that you are leaving us. How could you be so thoughtless? Watch out, they say sushi has worms in it." Another friend summed up the good feelings by saying, "Is the news true? I'm very excited for you."

We flew to Washington, D.C., the next day to prepare for President Clinton's announcement in the White House Rose Garden on Friday, June 11. So many friends were there whom we hadn't seen since we moved home to Minneapolis a few years before. Hillary Clinton graciously complimented me on my new suit, which had arrived by Federal Express, just in time. She made me feel quite welcome. During the ceremony, I realized that we were stepping back into public life, which meant renewed duties and responsibilities. Once again our lives would be scheduled. We would need a staff to help us carry out our objectives, as we had when Fritz was the vice president. But this time we would have to leave our family and friends to move to a foreign land, hoping to make a smooth transition into a culture so different from ours.

As I watched the ceremony, the fragrance of boxwood filled the air and I remembered all those happy times we had spent in the White House with Jimmy and Rosalynn Carter. I knew how honored Fritz was to serve our country once more.

LETTERS FROM JAPAN

President Clinton, Fritz, and Vice President Gore announcing the appointment before our friends in the audience and the press corps.

When the news became official, congratulations poured in. One friend sent a message, saying, "Now *omono* and *mama-san* must move to the land of rising suns, green tea, and lace doilies in the taxi cabs. There is a long tradition of Americans being smitten with Japan. My favorite is Lafcadio Hearn and his interpretation of country life." Another teased, "Bravo, Bravo, Bravo! All of us are very exited at the prospect of a cheap bed in Tokyo. Plus, I hear the Japanese are fond of lutefisk." A message from Maine read, "We need people like you in the limelight, making the news, setting standards, and creating excitement."

Haru Reischauer, the widow of my father's first cousin Edwin Reischauer, visited us in Minneapolis, bringing three books for us to read

Preface

before we left: *Japanese Business Etiquette*, *You Gotta Have Wa*, and a copy of her own book, *Samurai and Silk*, which traces the histories of both sides of her family, the Arai and the Matsukata heritages. She gave us lots of good advice, as did our predecessors, Mike and Bonnie Armacost (1989-1993) and the deputy chief of mission, Bill Breer, and his wife Peggy, who extended their stay in Japan to ease our transition into our new life.

Friends in Minneapolis kept asking, "When are you going?" Our friends in Washington, D.C., wondered, "When are the hearings?" Fritz concentrated on preparation for the appointment hearings before the Senate Committee on Foreign Relations in August. Mike Mansfield (ambassador to Japan from 1977-1988) joined us at the hearings, to our great pleasure. We were relieved when approval was given by the committee.

Later, I went back to Washington, D.C., to attend, with ten other appointees, the Ambassador's School sponsored by the State Department. After that, my work began—putting all but essential books and clothes into storage, mailing change-of-address cards, renting our house, and saying good-bye.

Next came the swearing-in ceremony on August 13 in the diplomatic reception rooms on the top floor of the State Department. Our Washington friends came with big smiles and warm hugs. Our eldest son, Ted, joined us as Vice President Albert Gore administered the oath of office and Secretary of State Warren Christopher confirmed it. Finally, we were official.

LETTERS FROM JAPAN

Vice President Albert Gore, Joan, Secretary of State Warren Christopher, and our son, Ted Mondale gather around Fritz after the swearing-in ceremony as the U.S. ambassador to Japan.

In all the preparations, it seemed as though I spent as much time making arrangements for our dog, Digger (a beagle–spaniel mix), as I did for Fritz and me. She was to fly separately, so after we had already left, our younger son William put her on Northwest #911, the flight that transports zoo animals, race horses, poisonous snakes, and beloved household pets. The pilot sent me a fax from Anchorage that Digger had eaten her dinner and had two nice walks. She arrived at Narita airport at 5 a.m. the day after we had come. She was then inspected by the airport veterinarian and released to my custody for the two week quarantine required by the Japanese government. Digger adapted

Preface

Digger waits patiently while I make arrangements with the Japanese immigration officials at Narita airport.

immediately to her new surroundings, loving the sights and smells of Tokyo. The only things she misses are the dip in Lake of the Isles on her daily walks, and chasing squirrels. (There are no squirrels in Tokyo. I think the big, black jungle crows must have ousted them.)

This book is a compilation of the columns I wrote for our neighborhood newspaper in Minneapolis, the *Hill & Lake Press*, from September 1993 to March 1997. The editors had asked me if I would be willing to write a monthly column for them. I was glad to have a way to share our experiences of living in Japan and seeing the country through the eyes of an ambassador and his wife.

LETTERS FROM JAPAN

•
This is my favorite picture of Fritz and me, walking in the garden of the ambassador's residence in Tokyo. My suit was made from a man's kimono I bought at a shrine sale.

September, 1993
Getting the Call

This is my calling card, or meishi, with my name and address in English on the other side.

"Welcome to Japan." Those words have been used to greet us by practically everyone we've met, accompanied by broad smiles and polite bows. We arrived on Northwest Flight 7 in the rain, a good omen to the Japanese. We learned that not everything goes according to plan here. Eighteen rice farmers refused to sell their land to the airport, built near the famous Narita temple, so there are some rice paddies on the grounds of the airport.

The deputy chief of mission, Bill Breer, and his wife, Peggy, met us. Both speak fluent Japanese. Peggy introduced me to three important connections: a woman vet (for our dog Digger), whose entire clinic is smaller than one examining room at the Kenwood Pet Clinic in Minneapolis; a beauty shop (no English spoken, but American Top 40 music is played); and a printer for personal calling cards, *meishi*, which everyone here exchanges.

To get around this city, a good sense of direction is vital, because the street signs are in non-romanized Japanese. So, instructions are given to turn right by the yellow-tiled building, go straight past the Kyoseki gas station, pass the shrine on the left, or turn left at McDonald's. Driving is difficult—traffic is almost impossible at rush hour and there is no place to park. And, of course, the steering wheels are on the right, so you drive on the left-hand side of the street. Luckily, Tokyo is a great city for walking, and the subway goes everywhere.

If you ever visit Japan, you'll probably want to bring home a souvenir. I should warn you that prices are unusually high here (for example, a cup of tea costs eight dollars). However, The Blue and White shop in the Azabujuban, a small neighborhood of quaint shops in central Tokyo, is charming. Amy Katoh, an American, scours the countryside to find craftspeople who use the traditional indigo dyes for fabrics; potters who use cobalt for their glazes and decoration; and a host of other crafts using blue and white

- **The first trip I took to visit a ceramic artist was to Mashiko, to see the studio of Jinai Sakata, who was preparing for an exhibition at the Takashimaya Department store in New York. Art Zegelbone, the embassy's cultural attache, and Greg Miller, a Macalester graduate and resident potter, sat on either side of me. Mr. Sakata was surrounded by his wife (at the end of the table) Tatsuzo Shimaoka's daughter (a glass blower) and Fusako Ishibashi, Art Zegelbone's assistant.**

September, 1993 *Getting the Call*

- Akebono was impressive; we felt very small standing next to him. Bill and Peggy Breer stand next to meet him. We didn't know it at the time, but the television cameras focused on us during the matches.

- Here is Fritz riding in the horse-drawn carriage with a Japanese official on his way to present his credentials to the emperor. You can see the 16 petal crysanthemum seal of the imperial family on the door.

themes.

On our first Saturday night here, the Breers took us to a sumo wrestling tournament to see Akebono, the Grand Champion. He is an American of Hawaiian ancestry and he towered above his competitor. The contestants sip some water from a long-handled bamboo cup and spit it out as an act of purification. They then throw a handful of coarse-grained salt into the ring for good luck. The matches are very short and very intense. To win, you have to push your opponent out of the ring of pounded earth. It looks easy, but it isn't.

Fritz presented his credentials to the emperor on Tuesday, September 21. He wore the traditional morning coat and rode in a horse-drawn carriage to the Imperial Palace. The emperor was up-to-date on events in the United States, and chatted with Fritz for at least ten minutes, when all he was required to do was to ask about President Clinton's health. Now Fritz is officially the U.S. ambassador to Japan.

Although we have just arrived, Fritz has flown back New York to participate in the meeting between President Clinton and Prime Minister Hosokawa.

We're off to a good start. The Prime Minister told Fritz that he liked pottery.

Sincerely,

Joan Mondale

September, 1993 *Getting the Call*

- I gave a birthday party for Mrs. Toshi Enomoto. She and Mrs. Joseph C. Grew, wife of the U.S. ambassador before World War II, were friends. Together they founded Nadeshiko-kai, a group of Japanese and American women who meet regularly to understand each others' cultures better.

From left to right on the back row: Jean Harris, Kristen Deming, Amy Katoh, Chako Hatakeyama, Miyuki Tamura, Reiko Ryuji, Yuri Konome, Amy Anzai. Front Row: Junko Enomoto, Joan Mondale, Mrs. Enomoto, and Haruko Hirasawa.

October, 1993
Making the Rounds

If you want to be lonely, don't come to Tokyo. We have been inundated with invitations to every imaginable event. The phenomenon reminds me of our days in the U.S. Senate in Washington, D.C., where dinner parties are an extension of the working day.

For those who like to go to luncheons, lectures, and classes, there are numerous groups to join: the Japan-America Woman's Club, the Women's Group of the Tokyo-American Club, the Tokyo-Washington Women's Club, the College Women's Association of Japan, the International Ladies' Benevolent Society, the Round Table, and Nadeshiko-kai, a social organization for women from the international community living in Tokyo and their Japanese counterparts. All have Japanese members, so I'm meeting wives not only of American businessmen, but also those of Japanese counterparts. At one tea, I met Princess Hisako Takamado. She lives in one of the Imperial Palaces. She teaches cooking to disabled adults in her kitchen once a week. Kayoko Hosokawa, wife of the prime minister, and Yasuko Hata, wife of the foreign minister, came as honored guests, also. Both were very outgoing and western in their manner and both spoke English. Mrs. Hosokawa had just come back from speaking in a prefecture (which corresponds to one of our states), urging

October, 1993 *Making the Rounds*

women to become active in politics. She had her own business and lived in Italy, until Morihiro Hosakawa convinced her to marry him and come home to Japan. Mrs. Hata told me of her recent visit to Boston to hear Seiji Ozawa conduct the Boston Symphony Orchestra. Seiji Ozawa was a high school classmate of her husband's. The two women obviously were friends and it reminded me of Fritz's impressions of how much President Clinton and Prime Minister Hosokawa had in common when they met at the U.N. in New York. They are both young; both had been governors; and they both were elected to make changes. However, our

•

A friend from Nadeshiko-kai invited us to watch a yabusame event. It was full of colorful costumes and pagentry. Yabusame means archery on horseback, performed as a competition. Samurai warriors rode on horseback to shoot arrows at targets in the late Heian and Kamakura periods (800-1330 A.D.). Ever since I had seen the nicks arrows had made long ago on the wooden doors of a shrine in Kyoto, I had hoped we could see a yabusame performance. Here is one of the contestantants, followed by his assistant and two of the shinto priests, who had pruified all the participants beforehand.

country is much more comfortable with change. In Japan, during the Tokugawa Shogunate, which lasted for more than two hundred fifty years, relatively few changes occurred.

The other day, I visited the Nishimachi International School, which the children of many foreign diplomats attend. The children use computers, starting in the first grade. It was amazing to watch American children chatting away in Japanese. I hope some of them will want to join the Foreign Service when they grow up.

I am struggling with the language. Try as I may to capture the intonations, I know my Minnesota accent shines through. However, I'll keep trying. I don't want to make the same mistake one American ambassador's wife made. She stood in the reception line at the Embassy, greeting guests by saying what she thought was "Good Evening" in Japanese, when, in fact, she was telling them to go home to bed.

Next week, Fritz and I are off to Kyoto, that wonderful, old city filled with temples, and the former home of the emperor.

Sincerely,

Joan Mondale

February, 1994
Art from America in Japan

"To be an ambassador" and "to entertain" are almost synonymous. Recently, Fritz and I gave a reception for those responsible for the exhibition of the Barnes Collection in Tokyo, sponsored by the National Gallery of Art. We invited a lot of artists. Jenny Holzer was among the guests; she was in Japan to give a lecture about her exhibition in Mito City. We talked about the 28 benches Walker Art Center had acquired at Christmastime, the gift of an anonymous donor. The granite benches, which have aphorisms chiseled into them, occupy an entire quadrangle in the Minneapolis Sculpture

Princess Tomohito chats with Rusty Powell, Director of the National Gallery of Art, while Prince Tomohito converses with Richard Glanton, Director of the Barnes Foundation.

Virginia Cartwright's "Folded Jar" and Thomas Hoadley's "Brown Florentine Bowl" were two of the porcelain works we borrowed from the Renwick Gallery of the Smithsonian Institution in Washington D.C..

Garden. She told me that she was moving from upstate New York back to Greenwich Village, where the grocer was right around the corner, her friends were close by, and she liked the sense of community she found there. If artists are our urban pioneers, then there is hope for the city in the long run.

The next afternoon, I went to the opening of the Barnes Collection in the Museum of Western Art in Ueno Park. It was jammed! (The show had broken all attendance records in Paris.) Princess Tomohito cut the ribbon. She wore a fitted raspberry wool suit, with a matching pancake-shaped hat tilted over one eye, as the Empress wears her hats. She spoke fluent English and asked Rusty Powell, the director of the National Gallery, many questions about Mr. Barnes. It turned out that Barnes, a wealthy American collector, had asked the artist William Glackens to go to Paris to buy art for him. Glackens did so and trained Barnes's eye for the work of Renoir, Cezanne, Matisse, and other late nineteenth-century artists. Barnes was a friend of John Dewey and shared some of his ideas about education. He wanted to educate the non-elite of Philadelphia; in order to see how successful he was in this endeavor, he restricted access to his collection, in Merion, Pa. He required visitors to make reservations in advance and to list their occupations. When James Michener visited the collection, he put down "steelworker" instead of "author." This so enraged Barnes that he hounded Michener for years afterward.

February, 1994 *Art from America in Japan*

• Dorothy and Roy Lichtenstein talk with Fumio Nanjo, the arts consultant who commissioned Roy's work for Shinjuku i-land.

• We gave a reception for Roy and Dorothy Lichtenstein when they came to supervise the installation of "Tokyo Brushstroke I" and "Tokyo Brushstroke II", examples of public art at Shinjuku i-land. The walls of our music room displayed his prints, which were inspired by Native American visual themes and the German Expressionist style.

• Akiko Kuno joined Red Grooms and me for dinner after his opening. She is the author of "Unexpected Destinations", the story of her great grandmother, who was the first Japanese woman to be graduated from Vassar College.

There are so many Minnesotans who have a Japanese connection. Weiming Lu, the executive director of the Lowertown Redevelopment Corporation in St. Paul, came to Tokyo to give a keynote address about urban revitalization at the Conference on the Future of the Cities. He took me to see the work of Koho Kato, his teacher and a master calligrapher, and the work of his students. Mr. Kato was dressed in traditional full, pleated brown *hakama* pants and a short *haori* jacket. He wore traditional *zori* sandals with formal, white *tabi* socks. He was warm and effusive. Weiming translated his explanation that the treatment of the kanji characters was close to crossing the line between calligraphy and painting. The powerful and expressive kanji were bursting with energy and feeling. The act of creating them joins the eye, mind, hand, and heart. A photograph of each artist accompanied the work and we saw that many of these huge, strong images had been created by housewives.

We receive all kinds of support from the United States. We are living in the Deputy Chief of Mission's Residence, an Art Deco house built in 1947. The main residence, an imposing, hotel-like building, is undergoing renovation. (Ambassador Mike Mansfield called it a firetrap.) Carleton Varney, who decorated the tables for many state dinners in the Carter White House, is doing the interior design for the private quarters upstairs. We hope to move in by May 1, 1995. Meanwhile, we are enjoying the collection of works on paper borrowed from the Print Study at the Walker Art Center, and photographs from the Minneapolis Institute of

February, 1994 *Art from America in Japan*

Here we are, watching a Noh play. Noh drama is an ancient theatrical form; the actors wear masks which denote their identity (men play women's roles). their movements are slow and stylized.

Arts. We also borrowed porcelain pots from the Renwich Gallery in Washington, D.C. We have recruited several volunteers to give guided tours to interested groups. Many guests have commented about how the art has brought the house to life. You can't remain oblivious to the prints of Motherwell, Lichtenstein, and Steve Sorman (who lives in Marine-on-St. Croix), nor the photographs of Tom Arndt, Lee Friedlander, and Stuart Klipper.

I'm off to Kamakura to see a Noh play. Then back to Tokyo for the opening of a show by Red Grooms in the Shinjuku Mitsukoshi department store.

Sincerely,

Joan Mondale

March, 1994
Off to Hokkaido

Fritz and I flew up to Sapporo, on Hokkaido, one of the four main islands of Japan. It looked as though we were landing in Hibbing, pine trees and snow everywhere. Sapporo was host to the winter Olympics in 1972. Their subway system was built for those events.

Before Commodore Perry and his black ships opened Japan in 1853, Hokkaido was sparsely populated by Ainu tribes. The Meiji Era government (1868-1911) hired Americans to set up agricultural schools and to develop the potential of the Japanese frontier. An association between the Japanese government and the Massachusetts Agricultural College (UMass at Amherst today) was established. Dr. William S. Clark and a team of specialists were sent to Hokkaido with two boat loads of dairy cows, beef cattle, corn, potatoes, and hops. They founded an agricultural college, which grew into Hokkaido University (which has 10,000 students today).

People in Hokkaido have very fond memories of Dr. Clark. His exhortation to his students, upon his departure for the United States, has become Hokkaido's unofficial motto. In the days before women were accepted by colleges or universities, his parting words were, "Boys, be ambitious."

A reminder of the Americans' contribution to Hokkaido's history is the famous clock tower in

March, 1994 *Off to Hokkaido*

downtown Sapporo. The clock was made in Boston. It is housed in the original Hokkaido University building. The clock's chimes have struck the hour uninterruptedly for 113 years. Also, the railroad system was created by J. R. Crawford, an American.

Fritz and I had separate schedules. I visited a pottery workshop in Otaru. There aren't many potters on Hokkaido, because the clay isn't elastic or malleable enough. I toured the Sapporo Factory, an example of adaptive re-use of buildings. It was an old brewery turned into an American-type shopping mall, with the original brick walls intact and old tools and beer-making equipment incorporated into the design.

Hokkaido is unique because it is so close to Russia. The ownership of the four islands to the north, the Kuril islands, occupied by the Russians since World War II, is a volatile issue. The right wing in Tokyo drive around in black vans with white kanji characters painted on the

This unomi by Shimaoka of Mashiko (Hamada's prize pupil) incorporates an oval decoration which marks Mashiko, and rope design which identify Shimaoka's work.

25

sides, and wave Japanese flags and shout slogans over the loudspeakers, demanding that the Russians return the islands. (Nobody pays any attention to them. They are just a minor irritant.) The Russian Sakhalin Island is just across the Sea of Japan from Hokkaido. The Japanese sell used cars to the Russians and they, in turn, go door-to-door selling king crabs. The price of one crab equals an average Russian worker's entire month's salary (10,000 yen or $100. U.S. dollars).

Fritz's interpreter returned to Tokyo with dried octopus tentacles, a delicacy, for the friends who took care of her dog while she was traveling with us. Frankly, I prefer red bean paste sweets.

Sincerely,

Joan Mondale

Tsuboya-yaki ware made by Eiyo Arakaki in Okinawa.

April, 1994
The Prime Minister Visits

Tokyo is the center of Japan. It has no rivals. It is a restless city and the lively art scene reflects this, with exhibitions of every sort, most of which last only two weeks. In the last month, I've gone to the opening of "Celebrating the Stitch," featuring American embroidery, applique, etc., on the seventh floor of the Tokyo Main Department store; American contemporary prints from the Gemini Press in Los Angeles at the Hara Museum; "New York: A Magnet for Artists," organized by the Brooklyn

- **The Hosokawas invited us to visit Kyoto with them. We stayed in Tawaraya, a famous ryokan. Each of us wore a yukata for breakfast.**

Museum at the Tokyo Metropolitan Art Museum; the opening of a new museum, the Ancient Mediterranean Museum (devoted to one man's collection—quite common here); and a show of David Smith at the Sezon Museum, organized by the International Sculpture Center in Washington, D.C. There I saw an old friend, David Smith's "Star Cage," which Martin Friedman had borrowed for the Vice President's House from the University Art Museum (now The Frederick R. Weisman Art Museum), when we lived in Washington, D.C. I've counted a total of two hundred museums in Tokyo. I'll never get to see them all!

We had a special evening the other night at the residence. Fritz invited Prime Minister Morihiro Hosokawa and his wife, Kayoko, for dinner, a week after the Prime Minister announced he was going to resign. (Fritz told him he had experienced a similar disappointment.) They brought five eggshell porcelain tea cups with nine blue circles, the family crest, on each one. Their family is a distinguished one which came to prominence as samurai warriors and later became *daimyos*, or feudal barons, in the fourteenth century. They were leaders accomplished in the arts, crafts, and writing, as well as military skills. The family maintains their extensive art collection today. I told them I would display the tea cups in my ever-growing collection of Japanese pottery, but Kayoko wanted us to use them. When the name of the new prime minister was announced, Hosokawa returned to the Diet, the Japanese parliament, and they moved out of the prime minister's official house, old and dark with no living room.

One of their daughters argued so successfully with a man who was criticizing her father with a bullhorn on a sound truck, parked outside of her school, that he drove away. I asked Kayoko what they would do when her husband was no longer prime minister. She said, "SLEEP!" We served an American meal; lamb chops and mint jelly, baked potatoes with sour cream, green string beans, and hot pecan pie with vanilla ice cream for dessert. Not a speck of food was left on their plates. Most of the conversation dwelt on the political realities of change. Hosokawa reassured Fritz that Japan would continue to move toward a more open economy. But much work remains to be done in this area. As the Hosokawas left, Kayoko smiled broadly and told me she was coming to hear my slide talk "Art in Public Places" at the Japan–America Women's Club luncheon.

I took Digger to be checked for heartworm. A black toy poodle came over to say "Hello" in the waiting room. I asked her owner what her name was. It was Hillary, which means smart and bright to the Japanese.

Sincerely,

Joan Mondale

P.S. I haven't listed all the museums of traditional Japanese art and crafts I've visited or the gallery openings of current Japanese artists' shows—too many to mention.

May, 1994
Okinawa, the Unique Island

I was surprised and pleased to hear that "welcome" is pronounced "Minnesota" on Okinawa. We visited the *urumajima*, or beautiful island, for an official visit. Fritz toured the military bases, which occupy 20 percent of the land, and I had a separate schedule to see potters, weavers, fabric designers, and glass blowers. The first thing you notice is how relaxed and easy-going the people are. The tropical climate and the turquoise water, palm trees, and lush mountainous jungles reminded me of St. Thomas in the Caribbean (with fewer roosters or rusty, abandoned cars) and of Hawaii. I had lunch with Shinman Yamada and his wife in the village of Yomitan. Thirty years ago, the town fathers realized crafts were dying out, so they decided to lease land to craftspeople and encourage them to move there. Yamada had done just that, when his neighbors in Naha City (the capital) had complained about his smoky kiln. He and three other potters built an *anagama*, a wood-fired, hill-climbing kiln, which they share. It looks like a giant mole hill, with peep holes into each chamber and a heavy tile roof to protect it. They don't use cones to determine the temperature inside the kiln as American potters do; they can tell by the color of the flames. I threw some pots for the TV cameras (Yamada was too shy to demonstrate) and we talked about his show in San Antonio, Texas, this fall. His house was

May, 1994 *Okinawa, the Unique Island*

• Potter Shinman Yamada and his wife enjoy a good joke at lunch, using the colorfully glazed pots he made, set on a table covered with an indigo dyed textile. All the cups, bowls, and plates were made of clay, except the soup bowls, which were lacquer, black on the outside and red on the inside.

• Mrs. Masahide Ota, the wife of the governor, Lynda Pedersen, Fritz's Administrative Assistant, and I made our own bingata stencils.

filled with weaving from Afghanistan, China, and Indonesia, as well as mud cloth from Mali. His functional stoneware pots were glazed and decorated with traditional folk patterns. He came from many generations of potters and remembers seeing Bernard Leach, the famous founder of the *mingei* artistic movement, when he was five years old.

Another potter, Eiyo Arakaki, showed me the coil method he used to make huge, unglazed storage jars of the tsuboya type. His son is an apprentice who has worked in the workshop for six years, but his father won't allow him to make the large pots yet. We had green tea, black sugar bars, and *sata andaji*, a traditional Okinawan sweet, which tastes like pound cake. Then, on to Eijun Shiroma's studio, a fourteenth-generation fabric artist, who showed me how *bingata* designs are made. Stencils are cut with an Exact-o knife, using a dried tofu bar as a cutting board. They are placed on the cloth. A rice paste is brushed on, over the stencils. The stencil is removed and the nonpaste areas are patiently brushed with colored dye. Then, the rice paste is washed off and the design stands out. The background is colored next by covering the newly decorated areas with more rice paste, the dye is applied, and the paste is again washed off. The designs are based on nature: tropical flowers, birds, and butterflies.

There is another type of weaving design, called *kasuri*, in which the silk threads are dyed before they are woven on the loom. The splash patterns look like ikat, from Indonesia. The wife of Governor Ota, who accompanied me, wore a

May, 1994 *Okinawa, the Unique Island*

bright *bingata* kimono for dinner and a subdued brown and white *kasuri* suit for the tour. (Her husband has appointed a record number of women to important posts in his administration.)

The Okinawans used to be governed by their king in the Ryukyu Kingdom. We toured the newly reconstructed Shuri Castle, which had been destroyed in World War II. It had brilliant cinnabar lacquered walls and columns. The only records of what it had looked like came from scroll paintings.

Sincerely,

Joan Mondale

- **Mrs. Ota and I pose in a kimono from her collection and a bingata kimono lent to me for picture-taking.**

June, 1994
Mashiko, Home of Mingei Potters

The Japanese have a saying, "We taste with our tongue and with our eyes." Recently, I had lunch in the pottery village of Mashiko in a restaurant called Enkyo (which means to feel comfortable around a circle). It was hidden away on top of a hill, outside of town. We had many courses. The most memorable were greens from the surrounding hills. They were prepared as *tempura*, or deep fried. We were served dried trout lily, fresh fiddlehead ferns, new shoots of the tare tree (*taranome*), torn umbrella (*yaburegasa*), and king of the mountain vegetables (*shiode*). We drank four different kinds of green tea, each accompanied with a sweet, because the tea was so bitter. And we were treated to the delicacy *yuba*, thin layers of tofu curd, which is rare because it requires such a tedious process to make. Many little cups, plates, and bowls were used and none of them matched.

Mashiko looks more like a traditional Japanese village, circled by rice fields and green hills, than any town I have yet seen. I was in Mashiko, made famous by the potter Shoji Hamada, to be filmed throwing pots at Tatsuzo Shimaoka's workshop (he was Hamada's prize pupil). Shimaoka had just fired a new *noborigama* kiln, and presented me with two teacups, called *hatsugama*, because they were from the first

June, 1994 *Mashiko, Home of Mingei Potters Tokyo*

firing of a new kiln. He said they cured heart trouble, too! (A *noborigama* is a wood-burning, hill-climbing kiln, but with many separate chambers. The pine, balsam, and spruce chosen for the firing have a lot of iron, so that when the wood ash fuses with the pot in the firing, it makes a celdon-colored glaze.) Incidentally, one of the gifted young potters in Mashiko is Greg Miller, a graduate of Macalester College, who was apprenticed to Shimaoka for a year.

Back in Tokyo, I went to a luncheon in honor of Mrs. Hata, wife of the new prime minister. She told me that she had married her husband because he had a nice, stable job working for the bus company. They had met at a garden party given by a mutual friend on a September afternoon, became engaged in October, and married in December. Their meeting closely resembled a blind date. If it had been arranged, it would have been called an *omiai*. A *nakodo*, or go between, would have been hired by their families to find a suitable spouse. Many women I have talked to, privately over tea at lunch, met their husbands through a *nakodo* and they said that they approved of the custom.

Sincerely,

Joan Mondale

This is a photograph of Tatsuzo Shimaoka in a pensive moment as a judge in Mashiko's International Ceramic Competition.

June 11-15, 1994
The Imperial State Visit to Washington

The emperor and empress of Japan came to the United States with all the ceremony a state visit requires. Fritz and I flew back to the States to be part of their official visit. We drove to Andrews Air Force base on a Saturday and lined up along a red carpet to greet their Majesties as they descended from a huge white Boeing 747, decorated with a large red sun, symbol of Japan. Protocol demands that you may not reach out to shake hands first; you must wait until they offer theirs. And, you may not initiate a greeting; you may only respond to theirs.

Then, at 10 o'clock on Monday, we attended the arrival ceremony on the White House lawn. Lots of military bands, even a Revolutionary War fife-and-drum corps playing "Yankee Doodle Dandy," entertained us while we waited for them to come by limousine, with the American flag and the Japanese flag flying on the front fenders. We listened to a 21-gun salute in the distance.

On Monday evening, June 13, President and Mrs. Clinton gave a white-tie dinner in the Rose Garden, under an air-conditioned tent. It was a fairyland, with tiny lights decorating the boxwood hedges on all sides. Red and pink damask tableclothes were matched by centerpieces of red and pink roses. Hillary Clinton used Nancy Reagan's red-banded place settings

June 11-15, 1994 *The Imperial State Visit to Washington*

Fritz and I greet Hillary Clinton and Her Majesty at the reception in the White House. We felt comfortable there, for we had spent many happy evenings at state dinners when Fritz was Vice President.

to complete the color scheme. The first course was quail. Mstislav Rostropovich played his cello for the after-dinner entertainment. Every guest was very pleased to be there!

The guest list was celebrity-studded. It included Rosalee and David McCullough (author of the Truman biography), Katherine Graham (president of the Washington Post Company), Oprah Winfrey, Barbra Streisand and Peter Jennings, Michael and Judy Ovitz, Jane Fonda and Ted Turner, Hume Cronyn and Jessica Tandy, plus many corporate leaders. Senator Bill Bradley and Ernestine (New Jersey), Senator Diane Feinstein and Dick Blum (California), Senator Danny Inouye (Hawaii), as well as Speaker of the House Tom Foley, chairman of the House

Foreign Affairs Committee Lee Hamilton, and his wife Nancy, and Congressman Norman Mineta, from San Jose, California, were invited.

I sat next to Secretary of State Warren Christopher. We talked about his childhood. He was born in North Dakota and when his father became ill, the family moved to California. His father died when Christopher was 13 years old. Warren Christopher delivered newspapers in the same neighborhood in Los Angeles where our daughter Eleanor is now living.

The day after the White House state dinner we had lunch in Blair House, just across Pennsylvania Avenue, where the guests of the President and First Lady stay. That night the Embassy of Japan gave a reception for all of Washington's famous, it seemed. The Empress wore a pale peach kimono with a wide brocade obi, a pale *obiage* (a scarf tucked into the top of the *obi*) and an *obijime* (a woven cord tied around the middle of the *obi*).

We said a formal good-bye on Wednesday morning. Her Majesty said to us, "We'll see you in Tokyo."

Vice President Albert Gore and Tipper invited us over to see the Vice President's House. It was nice to be back after 13 years. Tipper Gore has decorated the house to create a warm and welcoming feeling. She's doing a great job as Second Lady.

Sincerely,

Joan Mondale

July, 1994
Sumo, the National Sport

Sumo wrestling is a traditional Japanese sport. The first public appearance Fritz and I made when we arrived last September, was to go to a sumo match to watch the *yokozuna* Grand Champion, Akebono (an American from Hawaii). He is very popular.

During Golden Week, when four of five working days are holidays, my Nadeshiko-kai group was invited to a stable, where sumo wrestlers train, to see them practice and have lunch. The young men with black loincloths started first. There was a great silence through it all, broken only by the sounds of slapping of thighs and stomping of those lifting their legs from side to side, high in the air, and coming down hard. Then, the more experienced men in white loincloths practiced. Still, it was very quiet. The contests are very short, lasting up to four minutes. The goal is to push your opponent out of the *dohyo*, or clay ring, bounded by a circle of straw.

After a two hour session, they broke up into informal pushing contests, where one wrestler would push another backwards, sliding across the ring. Then, one would tap the other on the head or neck and he would fall down and roll over, like an acrobat. When I asked why they did that, I was told that they needed to practice falling without hurting themselves. Needless to

LETTERS FROM JAPAN

- The young wrestlers watch as the two others practice.

- Kimi Matsukata explains an aspect of the sumo world as a young wrestler serves *chanko* to us.

40

say, after the practice, the wrestlers were pretty much covered with clay. During this part of the practice, there were lots of grunts and shouts, which I was told were, "get along" and "hurry up." The wrestlers were clearly enjoying themselves. Some of them even smiled.

Then we had lunch made by the wrestlers themselves, called *chanko*. It was a stew of tofu, cabbage, greens, and whatever. The wrestlers served us, dressed in *yukata*, cotton kimonos with obi sashes.

The wrestlers get up at five a.m. and practice until noon. Then they eat the first of two meals a day, on the theory that they gain weight faster that way. The wrestlers are called *rikishi* and the "get set" position is called *shikiri*, where the wrestlers squat down and face each other, crouched forward, supporting themselves with their fists on the ground and glare fiercely at each other. (In a real match, they would drink ritual water to purify their mind and body and spit it out. Then, they would scatter a handful of salt to purify the ring.)

The stable was in Koto-ku, an old section of Tokyo, dating from the Edo period (1600–1868). One of the guests was Koto-ku's representative in the Diet, the Japanese parliament. He is the oldest member of the Japanese parliament (he is 84 years old). When he got up to speak, he reminded me of Hubert Humphrey. He clearly was enjoying himself, just as Humphrey had when addressing a crowd. He stretched out his arms, wore a big smile, and made everyone laugh. I didn't need to understand Japanese to see how he warmed the audience.

Many wrestlers come from Hokkaido and are recruited in high school. (One of the women in our group said she could smell the hair spray they use to keep their hair up in a top knot, tied by white paper.)

After it was over, we all went home on the subway. There were nine stops to Roppongi, where I got off and walked to the residence.

Sincerely,

Joan Mondale

P.S. The Japanese woman who explained it all to me was Kimi Matsukata. Grandfather Matsukata played baseball on the University of Pennsylvania's team. He introduced the sport to Japan. At the first game, there were only two hundred fans. That's all changed—now thousands attend.

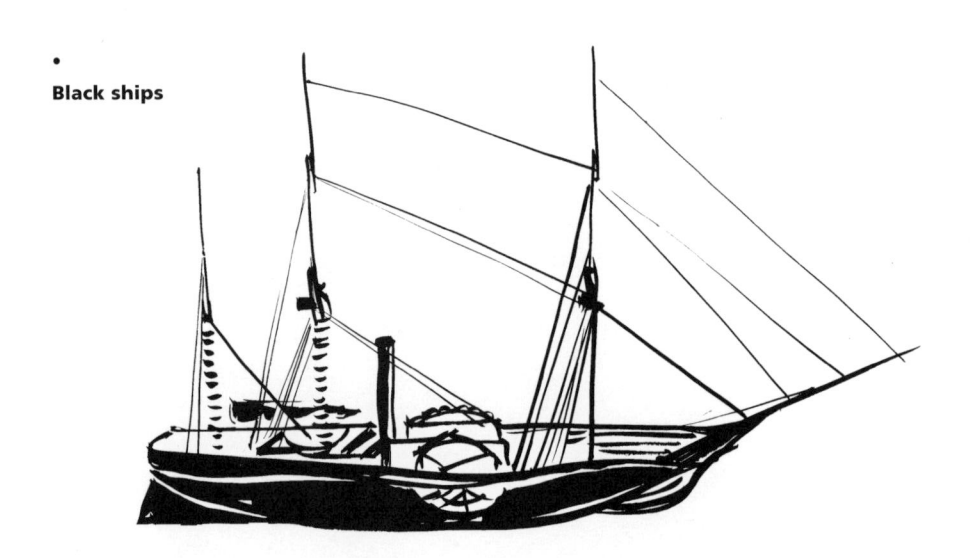

Black ships

September, 1994

The American Festival and the Carters Come to Town

Dorothy's ruby slippers.

The Smithsonian's impressive "American Festival" opened in Makuhari Messe, an enormous hall in Chiba, near Tokyo's Disneyland. Former president Jimmy Carter cut the ribbon and we trooped through the exhibition of everything imaginable from U.S. history. (It was a condensed version of the extensive collections in Washington, D.C.) Our history, culture, and diversity were illustrated by fascinating photographs of life in America, and different types of clothing, from Native American deerskin to football and baseball uniforms. Odds and ends of household appliances, life-sized models of suburban houses, and a scale model of the White House were on display. Our scientific achievements were well-documented by models of early automobiles, motorcycles, the Wright Brothers' "Vin Fizz" airplane and the space capsule that circled the moon. A space shuttle was there, with former astronauts ready to explain how it works. What I found most moving were the video of Martin Luther King, Jr.'s "I Have a Dream" speech on the steps of the Lincoln Memorial during the civil rights march of 1963, and a white Ku Klux Klan robe and hood; I also enjoyed seeing Dorothy's ruby slippers from *The Wizard of Oz*, the film clip from *I Love Lucy* showing Lucille Ball and Vivian Vance coping with the fast-moving assembly line of chocolate candies, and Commodore Perry's hat. (The commodore opened Japan to outsiders when his black ship arrived in Edo harbor in 1853, during the Tokugawa Shogunate. Following that momentous event, there was a period of growth and change known as the Meiji Restoration, when the city of Edo became modern Tokyo.) The Japanese co-sponsors of the exhibit were the *Yomiuri Shimbun* (a newspaper with a circulation of ten million copies a day) and NHK (Japan's public television station).

Jimmy and Rosalynn Carter stayed in Japan for a week, during which they climbed Mt. Fuji. They told us that the climb was longer and harder than they had imagined. In some places, the trail consisted only of white arrows painted on the black, volcanic rocks and they had to climb up on their hands and knees. It took them eight hours to go up and four hours to go down the other side of the mountain. They did it in

- **My first official speech was at the announcement of the coming of the American Festival to Japan.**

September, 1994 *The American Festival*

Commadore Perry's hat.

one day. They reported that it was much more difficult than climbing Mt. Kilimanjaro, which took four days to go up and two days to come down again. As they reached the summit of Mt. Fuji, the clouds disappeared and they could see for miles around.

You can't live in Tokyo and be oblivious of the crows. They are big, black Japanese jungle crows, about the size of a raven. They have a lot on their minds and discuss matters endlessly. They have chased the squirrels away, a big disappointment to Digger. One day, walking the dog, I found a crow's feather, measuring 13 inches long. It reminded me of the description of the ideal appearance of Japanese hair, "glistening black like a crow's wet feather."

Sincerely,

Joan Mondale

The Carters enjoyed a private, quiet dinner in our tatami room in the Deputy Chief of Mission's house, where we lived until the renovation of the ambassador's residence was completed.

October, 1994
Everyone Comes to Tokyo

When we returned to Tokyo from home leave on September 14, it was exactly one year after we first arrived. This time, everything seemed comfortable and familiar. We settled into our schedules with ease.

Accustomed to many visitors, we entertained the young and impressive publisher of *The New York Times*, Arthur O. Sulzberger, Jr., and his traveling party, for breakfast. J. Carter Brown, Director Emeritus of the National Gallery of Art in Washington, D.C., came for tea. He arrived on crutches, having broken both legs in Venice. He told me about the new arts cable channel called "Ovation", of which he is the chairman of the board. He had just had dinner with Stanley Hubbard on his yacht on the St. Croix River, discussing their cooperative venture. He told me that Evan Mauer, director of the Minneapolis Institute of Arts, had organized a small, temporary exhibition of sculpture borrowed from Midwest art museums for the White House including George Segal's *Walking Man* from the Minneapolis Sculpture Garden, and two Paul Manship sculptures from the Minnesota Museum of American Art, in St. Paul. These will be installed in the garden of the East Wing, which everyone who comes to the White House will see.

October, 1994 *Everyone Comes to Tokyo*

Earlier in the year, Ted Turner brought Jane Fonda to breakfast on a rainy Saturday morning. We had lunch with George and Helen Segal and Eiko Ishioka. Eiko won an Academy Award for her costume designs for Francis Ford Coppola's movie "Dracula". (She was quite spectacularly dressed in a black, full-length Issey Miyake skirt and a black, wrinkled oversize shirt. With her thick, black hair and fire in her eyes, she made her presence known!) Later, in the spring, a subdued and thoughtful Frank Stella, filled with

- Potter Toshio Ohi and his wife, seen on the right, came from Kanazawa, where he is the fourteenth generation potter of the Ohi family. They joined us when we entertained The Merce Cunningham Dance Company. Merce is standing to Fritz's right.

- Merce Cunningham clearly enjoyed eating *"udon"*, Japanese noodles.

47

LETTERS FROM JAPAN

- Mrs. Yoshiko Mori and the Kuroda Production Company were filming Warren MacKenzie in his studio the day before the announcement of Fritz's appointment as ambassador was made. It was hard to keep that a secret. We paused for a group photograph.

- Jack Lenor Larsen introduced me to several fiber artists in Tokyo.

48

October, 1994 *Everyone Comes to Tokyo*

ideas about public art, joined us for dinner one evening after his show opened.

Warren and Nancy MacKenzie are coming soon. Warren, a renowned potter, was invited to show a film on his life and work, and to lecture at the Mingei-kan, the Japanese Folk Craft Museum. This museum was established by Soetsu Yanagi, with encouragement from Shoji Hamada and Bernard Leach. In the 1920s, the three of them created the mingei movement, which combines Japanese and English craft traditions, with influences from the Yi Dynasty in Korea.

We are looking forward to greeting Bruce Dayton and Ruth Stricker in October. David Aaron, the U.S. ambassador to the Organization for Economic Cooperation and Development, is coming for OECD meetings here. (David was our foreign policy adviser when Fritz was a U.S. senator and vice president.)

Richard Koshalek, Director of the Museum of Contemporary Art in downtown Los Angeles (and trained by Martin Friedman at the Walker Art Center), will join us on November 4. He agreed to help me choose an exhibit of contemporary art from his museum for the newly renovated Ambassador's Residence, to be ready for us to move in on May 1, 1995. He received a grant this past year to take time off from his job to do as he pleased. So, he followed the Los Angeles Raiders football team. He went everywhere with the team and did everything except coaching. (He'll have lots of stories to tell!) NOTE: The Los Angeles Museum of Contemporary Art building was financed by a program which sets aside a ceratin percent of the construction costs and it was designed by the architect Arata Isozaki, whom we will invite to dinner, too. And on November 10, Jack Lenor Larsen, fabric designer, will bring us up-to-date on what's happening at the American Craft Museum in New York.

When we came back in September, we drove for one and a half hours from Narita airport into town. Once in our residence, we were treated to a hot meal-pasta with tomato sauce. When we tasted shrimp, squid, and octopus tentacles in the tomato sauce, we knew we were back in Japan.

Sincerely,

Joan Mondale

- **Onta-yaki teapot from Kyushu.**

November, 1994
Hakodate

There certainly are a lot of earthquakes around here. The other night the house began to rock, lampshades swayed, and the closet doors creaked. Digger didn't mind it a bit, but I did! After two minutes, which seemed much longer, the shaking stopped. It measured only a 3 on the Richter scale, but in Hokkaido (the northernmost island), the quake measured 7.9! I asked a wise Japanese friend what I should have done. She said, "Just pull the covers over your head and stay in bed. We think of an earthquake as a carp wiggling its whiskers."

The next week, when Fritz and I took a trip to Hokkaido, I found this message in my hotel room in Kobe: "Due to the stormy weather in this area today, there might be some squeaking noise in the guest room. The noise is caused by the flexible structure of this high-rise building. Thank you for your kind understanding. Signed, the General Manager." The general manager knew. The hotel room <u>did</u> squeak (not creak) that night.

Then, the next day, when we toured the waterfront in Hakodate, a seaport in southern Hokkaido, all the squid boats were docked. I asked why and was told that after the earthquake a typhoon was threatening Hokkaido and the fishermen couldn't go out to sea.

The squid boats were interesting. Down the center of each boat was a row of lights, covered with large glass globes. These lights attract the squid at night. Lines with hooks on them are cast out to catch them. When the lines are reeled in, the squid jump off into the bottom of the boat. We saw lots of dried squid at the farmers' market.

Hakodate was one of the two ports Commodore Perry opened when he came to Japan in 1853. Shimoda was the first, where the United States established a consulate. (The Japanese shogun refused to receive our consul general for eleven months.) Hakodate was opened because American whalers needed a port to take on coal.

The city reminded me of Duluth: hilly, windy, with the ocean everpresent. We saw the graveyard on a hill overlooking the bay where two of Perry's sailors were buried. We toured the old Russian Consulate, built of brick in 1910, and a perfectly preserved Greek Orthodox church with traditional woven-straw *tatami* mats on the floor. We stopped at a rice shop that had been in business since the Edo period. Several warehouses have already been gentrified into shopping malls, but the rest of the waterfront cried out for the James Rouse design touch.

Driving to the airport to fly back to Tokyo, we saw a perfect rainbow. Hopefully, it was signaling the end of bad weather.

Sincerely,

Joan Mondale

January, 1995
Kyushu

Fritz and I paid an official visit to Fukuoka, a port city on the island of Kyushu, one third of the major Japanese island chain. (The other islands are: Hokkaido to the north, with lots of snow; Honshu, where all the population is centered in the Tokyo–Nagoya–Osaka corridor; and then Kyushu in the south.) Kyushu is reached fastest by airplane. It is the island closest to Korea and traditionally has been open to foreign influences and change. (Today, new products are market-tested in Fukuoka.) Fritz went one way and I went another, to visit the home of sculptor Kiyokuni Kikutake and his wife, Michiko, a composer. Their son goes to Parsons School of Design in New York.

They were gracious, as Japanese are, and after looking at Mr. Kikutake's studio, we climbed up to the third floor of his house, perched on a hill, and paused for tea. We sat on Bertoia chairs (like those at Walker Art Center's Gallery 8 restaurant), drinking Japanese green tea in blue and white Danish porcelain cups with western handles. We ate persimmons grown in Fukuoka and talked about a mutual friend, Cissie Swig of San Francisco, who owns a piece of his sculpture and who is now the director of the Art-in-Embassies program in the State Department in Washington, D.C. I realized how much we had in common, even though we didn't speak the same language or even live on the same continent.

Thanksgiving dinner at our residence had brought us very close to home, when we invited students from Minnesota who were studying in Japan to join us that day. Fritz asked each to give their name, hometown, and university in Japan. Then he asked them what surprised them most about living here. One of the more insightful answers came from a student who said that the superficial adoption of some aspects of western culture, such as dress and music, hid an adherence to the traditional attitudes of an ancient culture just beneath the surface. He was studying and practicing *aikido*, the art of self-defense and self-cultivation, influenced by Zen Buddhism.

I visited an historic kiln in Arita on Kyushu's western shore, where extensive deposits of kaolin, which is used to make porcelain, are found. Arita ware was exported in response to the European demand for the blue and white porcelain first imported from China. When civil strife broke out during the Ming Dynasty (1368-1643), pirates roamed the trade routes, so China closed its seaports. Traders searched for other sources and discovered Arita ware. In the seventeenth century, Japan was closed to foreign trade, but the Dutch East India Company was allowed to occupy a small island, called Deshima, in Nagasaki's harbor. There, ten Dutch traders handled sales. (They brought their own cattle and pigs, because the Japanese

January, 1995 *Kyushu*

Left to right. Yasokichi Tokuda III, Kakiemon Sadaida XIV, Imaemon Imaizumi XIII. They are porcelain artists from Arita. Their pots were included in an exhibition at the Sackler Gallery in Washington, D.C.. We shared a good joke about potters wearing business suits.

didn't eat meat.) On that tiny island there was an Arita porcelain showroom, where orders were taken, to be delivered one year later.

Sakaida Kakiemon XIV, the fourteenth-generation Arita potter, showed me through his extensive studios, where the work done was specialized. I stepped inside his kiln, designated an "Intangible Cultural Property," which, by law, prevented him from changing or improving it, even though half of the pots coming out of the kiln had to be destroyed because of imperfections caused in the firing.

Later, I went to see another potter, Imaizumi Imaemon XIII, who showed me his collection. He had bought most of the porcelain at auctions in Europe and America, because, after all, they were export porcelain, not found in great numbers in Japan.

When Japan was opened for trade in the nineteenth century, Arita porcelain was shipped directly from the port of Imari, thus giving it another name, based on the addition of copper red, persimmon orange, and gold, which appealed to the Victorian love of lavish decoration. Factories were set up in Meissen, Germany, and in Delft in The Netherlands, to produce similiar ware.

I rejoined Fritz and we drove to Nagasaki to tour the western style house of Thomas Glover, a nineteenth-century Scottish entrepreneur who introduced shipbuilding, coal mining, and railways to Japan.

Sincerely,

Joan Mondale

February, 1995
Digger and the Crow

Digger was our only dependent abroad. We named our country house in Minnesota "Diggerwood" for her.

Digger, our dog, always likes a good chase. Since Japanese jungle crows, who are almost as large as ravens, have discouraged the squirrel population so thoroughly that there are no squirrels in Tokyo, Digger has been denied.

However, the other day when I was working at my desk in full view of our Japanese garden, which comprises the entire back yard, I saw an unusual occurrence. Digger was paying no attention when a crow flew down on the lawn a few paces behind her and began hopping sideways toward her. Digger turned, saw the crow, barked, and chased it away. Instead of escaping to the telephone lines high above the trees, the crow alighted on a low branch, just beyond reach. Digger turned away and the crow repeated the performance, flying down to the grass and hopping after the dog. On three separate days I observed this phenomenon. Was the crow teasing Digger or did the crow just want to play? No matter what the motive was, Digger liked the game.

Our Japanese garden is clipped and manicured and green all year round. But here and there are signs of the seasons. The first blossoms after winter appear on the white plum, an old, old tree, supported by bamboo crutches. Then the much-heralded and long-awaited cherry blossoms signal the arrival of spring. People go

We looked forward to the cherry blossoms each spring.

out to parks, temples, and cemeteries with picnic lunches (*obento*) and blankets to view the blossoms, much as we like to see our fall foliage.

All sorts of flowers blossom in turn after Golden Week, a string of holidays starting with Greenery Day on April 29, through Children's Day, May 5, when everyone who can leaves town. There are azaleas, wisteria, daphne, rose mallow, hydrangeas, and gardenias for summer. Then, camellias, roses, and chrysanthemums bloom almost all winter long. (The emperor's crest is composed of a 16-petal chrysanthemum.)

Every garden has a pine tree, the symbol of long life. Our garden has a little pond with seven carp. Digger likes to take a drink of water from

February, 1995 *Digger and the Crow*

Our daughter, Eleanor, visited Fusako-San and Terumi-San who took care of the DCM residence. They served as Digger's nurses when she became ill.

the *tsukubai*, a stone water basin traditionally set near the tearoom in a tea garden, where guests prepare for the tea ceremony by crouching down to wash their hands under the water which flows through a bamboo pipe.

There is a tiny minority of birds other than crows: ubiquitous sparrows and chickadees, with an occasional Asian species of azure-winged magpie, brown-eared bulbul (who peep instead of sing), and black and white wagtail (so named because their long, narrow tails pump up and down when they walk). Unfortunately, their cries are mostly drowned out by those of the crows, who keep up a steady conversation, often starting before dawn.

Sincerely,

Joan Mondale

March, 1995
Disaster in Kobe

The Kobe City earthquake lasted 40 seconds. Although it did no damage in the Tokyo area, it was the worst earthquake in Japan since the Great Kanto Plain earthquake of 1923, which leveled Tokyo and Yokohama. No one expected it. Kobe had rarely experienced a serious earthquake and only 6 percent of the houses had earthquake insurance.

Kobe was a beautiful city that many American expatriates chose as their residence. (Kobe may be best known to us for the famous beer-fed Kobe beef.) Eight thousand American businessmen, students, and retirees were living there. After the disaster struck, many walked for six hours to escape.

Aid came pouring in. American servicemen and their families at Yokota and Yokosuka bases personally contributed 25 tons of food and clothing. The U.S. government contributed blankets, water, and tents. Billy Joel donated the proceeds from his Osaka concert. Patrons of the Paul Taylor Dance Company, on tour in Japan, raised thousands of dollars from New York. And the new sumo grand champion (*yokozuna*) Takanohana donated one of his prizes—a year's supply of rice.

The quake spurred a new volunteer spirit as calls for aid inspired thousands to contribute

March, 1995 *Disaster in Kobe*

Fritz took this photograph out of the window of our car as we toured the extensive damage of the earthquake.

time and materials. For example, a group of 30 Japanese college students hiked for three hours from the nearest operating train station to a hard-hit area to help with the clean-up, to distribute food, and even to entertain the survivors.

Fritz was moved by an event reported by the U.S. Consulate in Osaka. Toshio Tanahashi discovered the body of an American teacher, Voni Lynn Wong, and recovered it from the wreckage of her home. He had stopped by, looking for someone else. Tanahashi reported his discovery and recovery of Wong's body to the U.S. Consulate and helped consulate staff break through the local city office's red tape to obtain a death certificate, which was necessary to transport the body back to the United States. (Northwest Airlines provided free transportation.) Only when all the work was completed, 12 hours later, did he reluctantly excuse himself, explaining that his house was uninhabitable due to the quake damage, and that he had to make arrangements for his own family for the night. It turned out that he had never met Ms. Wong.

Fritz and I went down to Kobe for two days to see how we could help. Poor people living in traditional Japanese houses suffered the most. The earthquake's tremor made a figure eight; the tile roofs rose and then fell, crushing the houses beneath then. Our consulate in Osaka and the compound housing the staff escaped damage, but left them without water or heat for two weeks. (The swimming pool saved them. They just filled up buckets of water to use for drinking and cooking, not enough for bathing.) Marines from nearby bases brought water for the survivors. Since there were no hotel rooms in which they could stay, the consul general housed them on the tenth floor of the Consulate. One group of Marines had driven for twenty straight hours, because the tunnels through the mountains were closed.

Sincerely,

Joan Mondale

April, 1995
Student Exchanges

One of Fritz's jobs as ambassador to Japan is to promote understanding between our two countries. An important way to do that is by encouraging students and teachers to study abroad. We have no trouble promoting study in the United States. Currently there are forty-seven thousand Japanese studying in our country, and we are very glad to have them. However, only seventeen hundred Americans are taking college courses in Japan. And, in all of Japan's 98 national universities, employing thirty-seven thousand full-time faculty members, fewer than ten American faculty are permanently employed.

Two reasons for this are obvious. Every Japanese schoolchild studies English. By the time they reach college, they can read and write it, but not all can speak English fluently. Unfortunately, very little Japanese is taught in the United States. Also, Japan is the most expensive country to live in worldwide. The language and the cost put Americans at a disadvantage.

Our colleges and universities are very attractive to students from around the world. We expect questions, criticism, dialogue, and debate. We welcome and make special arrangements for overseas students. Not so in Japan. Class discussions and questions are not tolerated. Suggestions for change are not considered, and

LETTERS FROM JAPAN

•
Another important part of Fritz's job is to hold regular briefings with American journalists reporting from Tokyo. His early morning breafasts were well-attended. Rust Deming, his Deputy Chief of Mission, sat to Fritz's right, two seats away.

many bureaucratic stumbling blocks hinder the progress of outsiders. For example, students from abroad must be financially guaranteed by a Japanese sponsor. Nonprofit organizations dedicated to student exchange are not tax-exempt, so they have difficulty raising funds and cannot sponsor students. College courses taken by foreign students are not recognized by major universities in Japan and our students are not eligible for standard benefits, like rail passes, available to all Japanese students.

64

Fritz is urging the Ministry of Education to ease some of its restrictions on students studying here. Among the proposals are increasing the budget for international exchanges, establishing junior year abroad programs at Japanese universities, and providing scholarships to increase the number of foreign students in Japan.

For our part, we need to do more as well. Education is an area that presents tremendous opportunities for cooperation. In many ways the U.S.–Japanese relationship is very solid, as Fritz has said: "Today, our two countries are partners in maintaining peace in the Asian region, in supporting democracy and human rights, in stemming the proliferation of nuclear weapons, in preserving the environment, and advancing the frontiers of science." It would be even better if our cooperation at the official level were supported by a growing number of American and Japanese students studying in each other's lands.

Sincerely,

Joan Mondale

May, 1995

*Iwo Jima, the Sulphur Island,
50 Years Ago*

The famous photograph of U.S. Marines raising the American flag on Iwo Jima will always be the most vivid reminder of World War II in the Pacific. The Iwo Jima monument in Washington, D.C., continues to be an ever-popular tourist attraction. *Iwo* means sulphur and *jima* means island.

Fritz and I went to the ceremonies commemorating the fiftieth anniversary of the bloodiest of battles on that tiny island. (It is only eight square miles.) Over eight hundred American veterans, most white-haired, some bent and creaky, attended the solemn occasion. Japanese veterans came, too. One of the more compelling voices was that of Mrs. Kuribayashi, the widow of the Japanese commanding general. She and her daughter were dressed in black. Her daughter helped her step up to the podium and supported her as she delivered her heartfelt message in a high-pitched voice, with obvious sincerity. She said, in essence, that the peace of today has been built on those souls who gave their lives here. She had told us beforehand that her husband had lived in the United States for seven years and that we had been very good to him. He was very unhappy to have to fight the Americans, when we entered the war.

Afterwards, Fritz and I went down into the caves which were connected by tunnels

May, 1995 *Iwo Jima, the Sulphur Island, 50 Years Ago*

throughout the island. They were filled with the debris of living: old, rusted tea kettles, broken rice bowls, water canteens, and stacks of shell casings. We saw and smelled the sulphur rising out of holes in the ground. We climbed Mt. Suribachi, the place where the flag was planted. Entrenched Japanese gunners on the mountain had a commanding position over our troops, who landed on a beach of black, volcanic sand into which they immediately sank, troops, tanks and trucks alike. It took four days for the Americans to move off the beach.

Iwo Jima was important strategically, because it provided a landing strip for crippled bombers. It took 36 days to secure the entire island, so planes had to land and take off amid Japanese gunfire at one end of the runway.

•
This is the view Japanese soldiers had from Mt. Surabachi where wave after wave of our troops landed on the volcanic sand of the beach.

We encountered some of the usual diplomatic difficulties when a Navajo veteran left his passport at home in Arizona. (He had served as a "Navajo Talker." His native language had never been written, so he could send messages that the Japanese had no hope of understanding.) He wasn't the least bit concerned about his missing passport. He blithely announced that he hadn't needed a passport when he came to Iwo Jima the first time and he didn't see why he needed one now! (One of our foreign service officers from Okinawa brought along proper papers and the U.S. official seal in case other passports were lost.)

Everyone had a story. Retired Lieutenant General Snowden told of diving into a crater on the beach during a Japanese zero attack. A zero's guns were stationary at the tips of its wings. As one of the planes flew over, knowing he was safe, he smiled and waved at the pilot. The zero circled and made another run at the beach. This time, the Japanese pilot smiled and waved.

At the Japanese shrine, we met a member of the Diet, the Japanese parliament, whom Fritz knew. (All Diet members wear in their lapels a small maroon button with a tiny gold chrysanthemum in its center, which indicates their office. This makes it easy to identify them!) The two men exchanged a few words (I'm always thankful for our interpreter) and then the Diet member turned to me and started talking about pottery. He invited me to the opening of a show of a potter friend of his in the prefecture he represents.

May, 1995 *Iwo Jima, the Sulphur Island, 50 Years Ago*

As the sun set, we wandered around a huge airplane hangar, chatting and nibbling on sandwiches, waiting to be flown back to Okinawa and then to Tokyo. Fritz was surrounded by veterans from all over the country who wanted to tell their stories, too. Several had come from Minnesota.

We all agreed that remembering the war and all who died helps us keep the peace.

Sincerely,

Joan Mondale

- **Every winter, palm trees are carefully wrapped with straw to protect them from snow and cold weather. The climate in Tokyo is similar to that of North Carolina.**

June, 1995
At Last, Our Own Home

We have just moved into the newly renovated Ambassador's Residence up the hill from the Embassy in Tokyo. Completed in 1930, it was the first residence designed and built by the U.S. government as an Ambassador's Residence anywhere in the world.

- **Maureen Murphy, an interior designer in the U.S. Department of State, planned the renovation of the residence. She wanted to recreate the decor of the 1930's, so she visited the Biltmore Hotel in North Carolina to absorb the flavor of the eclectic style of that era.**

June, 1995 *At Last, Our Own Home*

This is the view visitors have when entering through the front door. Fritz and I customarily stood on the marble floor with the black and white squares to greet out guests. Often, Keiko Shiga would make a huge floral arrangement to signal special significance to the event.

All the famous ambassadors lived here: Joseph Grew, who stayed for ten years (from 1931 through the start of the war), General Douglas MacArthur, Edwin O. Reischauer, and our longest serving ambassador, Mike Mansfield.

Much of the history of U.S.–Japanese relations was played out in this residence, including the famous visit of Emperor Hirohito to General

MacArthur, shortly after Japan's surrender in 1945. The photograph of that meeting was on the front page of nearly every newspaper in the world. (When Joseph Grew spotted some of his Arita porcelain in the background of the photograph, he wrote General MacArthur asking for its return.)

When the United States entered the war after the Japanese attack on Pearl Harbor on December 7, 1941, the Joseph Grew family and many of his staff lived in the house for six months, until they were allowed to return to the United States on the Swedish steamliner *Gripsholm*. They lived in isolation and had nothing to do, so they called the living room "The Lido" and entertained themselves with card games and contests. Their drying laundry hung everywhere.

- **The official work of our mission is carried on in the American Embassy in Tokyo where Fritz's office is on the ninth floor. All he had to do was walk down the hill to work each day.**

June, 1995 *At Last, Our Own Home*

There is an oil portrait of George Washington here. When General MacArthur entered the residence in the fall of 1945, he saluted the portrait and said, "General, it's been a long time, but we made it."

The residence was designed by an American architectural firm, Van Buren Magonigle of New York, which hired an American architect residing in Tokyo, Mr. Antonin Raymond. (He had come here to help Frank Lloyd Wright design the Imperial Hotel.) The building was recently described as "an engaging mongrel," because it defies classification. It was built for entertaining. It has a huge living room, a spacious dining room (when you smack your lips, it echoes), a gorgeous formal garden, and lots of marble. The State Department planned

• This is the formal living room with chairs and tables arranged in conversational groupings.

the interior design in the spring of 1993, long before we arrived. The living quarters upstairs benefits from the magic touch of Carleton Varney, president of the design firm Dorothy Draper, Inc. The downstairs is serious and formal, while the upstairs is a lot of fun. When the artist Frank Stella climbed the sweeping staircase, he said the upstairs reminded him of Miami. (There will be an article about the residence in *The Architectural Digest* in September.)

We were sad when the works on paper from the Walker Art Center and the Minneapolis Institute of Arts had to be taken down and returned. We will miss them, for they brought the Deputy Chief of Mission's House to life. Richard Koshalek, director of the Musuem of Contemporary Art in Los Angeles has lent a collection of mostly cutting-edge work by Los Angeles artists. Frank Gehry's *Fish Lamp* greets our guests and reminds us of his gigantic fish in the conservatory of the Minneapolis Sculpture Garden. Robert Rauschenberg's 10 prints of *Dante's Inferno* puzzles visitors as they enter the residence. Jim Dine's bathrobe painting, *The Yellow Robe*, and Chuck Close's portrait of composer Philip Glass are paired in the loggia. Los Angeles color photographer Richard Prince has four re-photographed ads for overstuffed furniture in the living room and Max Yavno's black and white studies of poor people in L.A. at work or in repose enliven the dining room. Llyn Foulkes's ominous *Postcard #8*, Jack Goldstein's powerful *Rooftops*, and Mitchell Syrop's pop poster *Screen Test* bring the L.A. touch of transformed appearances.

June, 1995 *At Last, Our Own Home*

We have recruited ten volunteer guides to conduct tours of the art in the house, in both English and Japanese. Many groups have already signed up and interest is mounting.

For our first large-scale reception, we entertained 350 workers from the Obayashi Company, which had done the renonvation on the residence. Many brought their wives (which is not normally done) and proudly showed off their workmanship. (I liked shaking their roughened hands. The marble workers were the best.) As a symbol of our appreciation, we presented Fritz's hard hat, with "Ambassador" printed on it, to the artist who stencilled walls and applied gold leaf to the ceilings. The construction company, in turn, presented the

- Jack Goldstein's "Untitled (Rooftops)" provided a commanding presence in the dining room. It reminded me of impending disaster with the bright lights in the background suggesting an explosion and the tornado shape on the left signaling powerful winds. It could have been a dream.

75

house with a large porcelain pot made by the thirteenth-generation potter, Imaemon Imaizumi, from Arita. It stands on the coffee table in the library.

Fritz says that public housing isn't so bad, once you get used to it!

Sincerely,

Joan Mondale

P.S. Before we moved in, we held a reception for Macalester alumni, honoring President Bob Gavin and his wife, Charlotte. After eleven years of leadership at Macalester, he has announced that he is stepping down. He will be missed. It was the largest alumni gathering outside the Twin Cities.

- **The indigo dyed kasuri placemat was made from a kimono. The napkin was once part of a blue and white cotton yukata.**

June, 1995 *At Last, Our Own Home*

It takes a staff of ten to keep the residence running smoothly. Everyone spoke Japanese and English and worked together as a team. Left to right: John Wastcoat, Miho Arisato, Yasuto Aoshima, Chako Ichida, Yuji Yonemitsu, Ryuichi Imai, Mitsuyoshi Sawano, Miyako Kato, Keiko Shiga, and Imre Hegedus. Miyako Kato was a superb organizer and mother hen.

Here are our volunteer guides at a luncheon I gave to thank them. Leftside of the table: Akiko Ueyama, two guests, Li Lundin, Junko Koito, Reiko Nagase. Right side of the table: (hidden) Yoko Haruhara, Janet Katano, Marion Lewis, Sue Stoddard, Sang-mi McHale, Keiko Shiga. The guides toured 107 groups of 1,392 visitors from May, 1995 through Nov. 1996.

July, 1995
WCCO-Radio Comes to Call

BY WALTER F. MONDALE
Guest Columnist

- **This is the kanji *kotobuki*. It means longevity and congratulations. It is widely-used calligraphy, found in restaurants, on festive decorations, and on gift wraps for weddings, births, and birthdays. It has become familiar and easily recognized to the non-Asian eye.**

We had a wonderful time with the WCCO "Good Morning" radio team who came to Tokyo for a three-day broadcast from Japan. Our old friends, Charlie Boone, Dave Lee, Rob Hahn (producer), and Dan Rowbotham (engineer) did a marvelous job. Joan and I love being here, but we are homesick for Minnesota. Those three days helped to remind us of home and of the many important connections there are between Minnesota and this fascinating country.

The theme of the series was the connection between Japan and the United States. There are many: religious, business, sports, diplomatic, military, educational, and cultural.

They interviewed Father Neal Henry Lawrence of St. Anselm's Priory, which is of the Benedictine Order, headquartered in St. John's University, Minnesota. Father Neal was in the invasion force taking Okinawa in World War II. He has spent much of his life since as a religious and educational leader here. St. Anselm's is one of the more prominent Christian institutions in Japan. Leaders from St. John's are often here.

They interviewed Shane Mack, formerly with the Twins and now with the Yomiuri Giants, one of Japan's leading baseball teams. Shane Mack described how baseball is played here and sent back messages to his friends on the Twins team.

They also interviewed Akebono, a champion (*yokozuna*) sumo wrestler. He is an American from Hawaii and a very nice and entertaining person. He is also HUGE! He weighs over 400 pounds! They interviewed him at his stable—the place where sumo wrestlers train and eat and eat! When asked what they eat, Akebono joked that they eat "see food." That is, when they see food, they eat it.

They interviewed several people heading Minnesota businesses here: Susan Marvin (interviewed from Minnesota), as well as Tsuo Hatsuda and Ichi Matsushima from Marvin Windows; Lowell and Cheryl Jacobson from Medtronic; and Frank Klare from the Radisson Hotel, located near Narita Airport. They talked with three Minnesotans at the embassy: Larry Farrar, from White Bear Lake, who is Minister Counselor of the political section, and Catherine Otto and Julie Snyder of the commercial and agricultural offices.

There is a large U.S. military presence here and they interviewed my military attaché, Commander Steve Fitzgerald, who will become the commander of the Naval ROTC at the University of Minnesota, starting this fall. Dr. and Barbara Chambers, from Willmar, who is in the medical corps, and Sergeant John Killoran from St. Paul, now assigned to Yokota Air Force Base, were also interviewed.

In addition to these interviews, they did a number of reports on the high prices in Japan ($100 cantaloupes!), a hilarious taped conversation with Dave Lee trying to buy a hamburger in English from a Japanese employee who obviously didn't know what he was talking about, a recording of an off-key singer showing off his skills at a karaoke bar, along with interviews with experts on Japanese popular music.

Above all, they proved their point: There are an astounding number of connections between Japan and Minnesota, including Northwest Airlines, Honeywell, Cargill, Anderson Windows, Cray Computers, and a host of others. Talented Minnesotans are to be found throughout Japan.

Joan and I talked about living in our newly restored residence, which for 65 years has been at the center of U.S.-Japanese relationships. Joan took them on a tour of the art and I talked about the fascinating history of this house. General Douglas MacArthur lived here for five and a half years. We learned that he was notified that he had been fired by President Truman while having lunch with the president of Northwest Airlines. It was here, in the living room, that MacArthur met Emperor Hirohito in that famous meeting, recorded by the photograph of the two of them, which appeared on the front page of almost every newspaper in the world.

We enjoyed their visit here and didn't like to see them leave.

There is a very impressive Minnesota State University at Akita, called MSU-A. It is a branch campus directed by officials at St. Cloud State University. Three students—Tara Kishel

July, 1995 *WCCO-Radio Comes to Call*

and Tom Anderson from Minnesota, and Naoki Hiabayashi from Japan—told about their unique experiences. Naoki will be attending Mankato State University this fall.

Sincerely,

Walter F. Mondale

•

Fritz and I pause a moment to look at the pots we've brought with us to show America's best. Left to right: Peggy Malloy, Paul Soldner, Peter Kaiser, Warren MacKenzie, Toshiko Takaezu, Warren's bottle, and the small square bottle was a gift from Tatsuzo Shimaoka, when I visited him in Mashiko.

September 2, 1995
Questions

Fritz and I have been in Tokyo for two years and wherever we go, we are asked certain questions. The first question everyone asks is, "Do you like living in Japan?" Our answer is always, "Yes, we both enjoy living there."

Being a potter, I especially like living in a country in which clay is so appreciated. Everyone, it seems, (men as well as women) performs the tea ceremony, with bitter green tea and lots of ceremonial moves. Each person has his or her favorite type of pottery to use in the ceremony, so I find it is easy to get a conversation started with strangers.

I am particularly happy because I have been asked to speak about art in public places all over Japan. The Japanese are interested and we have a thirty-year tradition of public art in the United States. I am going to include slides of Minnesota's newest public art project, that of Minneapolis-based Andrew Leicester's at the Minnesota History Center in St. Paul.

The second question we are asked is, "How long will you be there, or when are you coming home?" We point out that our appointment is "at the pleasure of the President," so we might be on our way home now!

The third question is, "Are you studying Japanese?" Although we have learned some

September 2, 1995 *Questions*

conversational phrases, we are not studying Japanese. Fritz has a full-time interpreter, who is excellent. When I need someone to translate, there are several people I can call upon. Foreign service officers who are assigned to Japan are required to spend two years, six days a week, eight hours day, studying the language before they are posted at the embassy.

The fourth question is, "How often do you come home?" We come home twice a year, in August for home leave and in December for Christmas. In addition, Fritz attends meetings in the United States when the President meets the Japanese Prime Minister.

Eventually, we find that nearly everyone we know has a direct or indirect connection with Japan. For example, the farmer in Scandia, from whom Fritz buys corn, tomatoes, green beans and cantaloupes, fought in the Battle of Okinawa. This summer, people from Nagasaki came to St. Paul, as part of the oldest American sister city relationship with Japan.

Fritz and I look forward to attending the opening concert of the Minnesota Orchestra, conducted by Eiji Oue. It reminded us of the close relationship that has developed between the U.S. and Japan through both our nations' love of music.

Sincerely,

Joan Mondale

•

Shunto Kato supervised my efforts in his studio. He is a master potter from Seto, a city outside of Nagoya known for its commercial porcelain products. Later, I glazed some of his teacups (*unomi*) which he fired in his kiln and sent to me. He had received one of my pots, made in Warren MacKenzie's studio in Minnesota. My pots made good presents when I travelled to visit artists and craftsmen in their studios or mayors and other city officials.

October, 1995
*Eiji Oue - Japan and Minnesota;
Settling into the Residence*

Eiji Oue, the Minnesota Orchestra's new music director, has brought a lively enthusiasm to the 93-year-old institution. Nicky Carpenter, chairman of the board, invited us to the opening subscription concert in Orchestra Hall when we were home in Minneapolis. Fritz gave a short greeting on stage. He recounted a comment a columnist made upon his appointment as ambassador to Japan. The journalist wrote, "You'll do just fine, because Minnesotans and the Japanese share a quiet arrogance." The audience burst into laughter at the thought.

Eiji Oue was chosen after an eleven-month search. There were four musicians from the orchestra on the search committee and they kept hearing from other musicians about how they liked Eiji Oue. One snowy evening, he conducted "The Nutcracker Suite" here as a substitute guest conductor. The musicians loved how he conducted that familiar piece of music.

After the concert, we went backstage where he greeted us, wearing a *uwappari* (pronounced "oo-wa-pari"). It is a short jacket, tied on each side, which is traditionally worn by men in the countryside. He greeted us warmly; his formal Japanese bow had all but disappeared as he hugged the women and shook hands with the men. We will always remember that spectacular concert. We will also remember the photograph in the newspaper of Oue wearing a Viking helmet, complete with horns and long blond braids.

The next morning, we returned to Tokyo to the renovated Ambassador's Residence, up the hill from the embassy. It had been photographed for the October issue of *Architectural Digest*. Many people asked us whose pots were those on the coffee tables in the living room—Warren MacKenzie's, of course! I have a small collection of contemporary American pots which enliven the serious, formal living room. It is the room where General MacArthur received Emperor Hirohito after the war. Our volunteer guides

- Nancy MacKenzie, a fiber artist, drew this sketch of our front door as a bookplate for books written by or about U.S. ambassadors to Japan in the library.

- This is the front door upon which the library's bookplate is based. Fritz's driver, Mr. Suwa, with his back to the camera, talks with Nakada-san, Fritz's bodyguard.

report that everyone asks about the American pots, because the Japanese have a high regard for clay. One of the reasons they do is the important tea ceremony, in which stoneware pots (not porcelain) are used.

Since we moved into this residence in April, I was struck by the fact that there seemed to be no record of previous ambassadors. So, I am starting a library of books written by ambassadors or about them; I'm hoping to receive donations, and will scout secondhand bookstores when we're on home leave next August. I'm also starting a scrapbook with whatever I can find about other ambassadors assigned to Japan.

President and Mrs. Clinton come to the Asian Pacific Economic Cooperation (APEC) meeting in Osaka in November. They will meet the Imperial Family and spend a few days in Tokyo. There will be lots of preparations for their visit. We are looking forward to seeing them again.

Sincerely,

Joan Mondale

November, 1995
Izu, Peninsula of Earthquakes

Mrs. Teiko Utsumi, of the Mingei-Kan, was a walking encyclopedia of knowledge about Japanese crafts.

In Japan, you never know exactly what's going to happen next. Mr. Oyamada, the young proprietor of the Petite Hotel Gekijo, a bed and breakfast in Izukogen on the Izu peninsula, invited me to his forest theater to introduce the film *Mingeisota*, about Warren MacKenzie. Teiko Utsumi, the program director of the Mingei-kan, the Japanese Folk Craft Museum, accompanied me to translate our conversations into English. We took the Odoriko express train. Two hours later, when we arrived at the very contemporary inn, Mr. Oyamada explained that Izu was a "nest of earthquakes," a mountainous range of resting volcanoes stretching from Mt. Fuji through Hakone (site of an open air museum) to Izu. He said the residents are relieved when the tremors occur because that means the energy has been deflated and they feel safer. We weren't disappointed, because just before I stood up to speak, the earth trembled, as it did again after I sat down. (The night before there had been thirty quakes!)

The next morning we giggled at the thought of visiting the Teddy Bear Museum, opened last April. It was a surprise —one thousand teddy bears arranged in various tableaux (*Swan Lake*, *The Christmas Carol*, *E.T.*, etc.). Many exhibits were mechanized by David Spaeth, an American who does the windows every Christmas for Lord & Taylor and Saks Fifth Avenue in New

November, 1995 *Izu, Peninsula of Earthquakes*

I have never seen so many Teddy bears at once! The motto of The Teddy Bear Museum is : "Happiness is a cute collection of Teddy bears who love to make people smile."

York. The director said the idea of the teddy bear came from a 1902 column and cartoon in *The Washington Post* about President Teddy Roosevelt's attempt to stop the shooting of bear cubs. Teddy's bear is the name which is remembered. In 1907, one million bears were sold. And the publication of *Winnie the Pooh* in 1930 fueled children's appetite for more stuffed bears.

The shape of the bears has remained pretty constant, but the materials have changed. Originally the bears were stuffed with straw and covered with mohair; in 1950, synthetic fibers were substituted. However, Monty and Joe Sours, who live in Montana, raise their own goats and harvest the mohair to make one-of-a-kind teddy bears. The only part of the bear that they buy are the buttons for eyes. We finished the tour, just as busloads of Japanese tourists descended upon the museum.

We drank green tea in *raku* bowls and ate lunch with potter Hitoshi Abe at his 400-year-old house, complete with a thatched roof, an *anagama* (hill-climbing kiln), and a Zen Buddhist meditation hall. He served *kiritanpo*, a stew made of rice and vegetables grown locally—mushrooms, watercress, *gobo* (a carrotlike root), *ito konnyaku* (speckled, transparent noodles)—and cooked over charcoal. It was delicious! A special treat were the river trout, caught by Hitoshi Abe himself. To eat them, you take the head and tail off, squeeze the body and pull out the bones intact. You are to eat the intestines, a great delicacy. They were bitter.

A stop at a neighbor's house revealed contemporary Italian blond *trompe l'oeil* furniture complimented by his wife's quilts, made of scraps of their grown children's and her maternity clothes, based on traditional American quilt patterns. We visited the Zen Buddhist Shuzenji Temple, built in 807 A.D. Its long history includes many fires, lots of intrigue, and several political murders.

Our train back to Tokyo was cancelled because of the threat of earthquakes, but all we had to do was exchange our tickets for a local train, and then transfer to the *shinkansen*, or bullet train. We arrived safely in Tokyo only five minutes later than expected.

Sincerely,

Joan Mondale

December, 1995
Women in Japan

It's interesting living in what is commonly perceived by westerners as a male-dominated society in which women are separate and unequal. I was invited to speak about American women at Kokugakuen Junior College in Takikawa City, a one-and-a-half hour's drive north of Sapporo, on the island of Hokkaido. The leaves had changed to brilliant reds, yellows, and browns (they hadn't changed yet in Tokyo) and the landscape reminded me of the drive up north in Minnesota in October. I spoke to the students in the gym, decorated with flags of many nations for International Communications Day.

The questions that followed my speech were thoughtful and reminiscent of questions so often asked by American women. Should women retain their maiden names? How do women balance careers with traditional roles as caregivers? Who will take care of the children? What are the remedies for sexual harassment? How can one person make a difference?

After the formal program, we went to the Ghengis Khan restaurant for a traditional Hokkaido dinner of lamb and vegetables, cooked on a burner at each table. Four women were seated with me: Kuniko Davidson, a Japanese married to an American foreign service officer; Fumie Ozaki, a high-ranking adminis-

trative official in the city government; Waka Watanabe, a member of the Takikawa City Council; and Dr. Carol Browning, a professor at the college from Salt Lake City, Utah. Carol opened the conversation by asking why Japanese women didn't use dishwashers (or clothes dryers). Kuniko Davidson said that dishes used for meals were odd sizes and the rice was sticky and wouldn't come off. Also, there wasn't any room in Japanese kitchens and people weren't accustomed to using them. Besides, it was a woman's job to do the dishes by hand. The other Japanese career women agreed with her. Kuniko added that she was glad to be a housewife, expecting her first child. After college, she had been hired by the public relations department of NTT, the telephone company, which had a reputation for being considerate of its female employees. However, she soon found out that part of her job required her to accompany her boss after work to karaoke bars and to pour beer for him and his male colleagues. So, when she married, she quit her job—knowing there would be pressure for her to leave anyway and, should she become pregnant, she would be fired. Apparently, there are no remedies, short of lawsuits, against employers. Grievances are hard to prove in a climate where a woman's place is generally seen as in the home. They explained to me that in fairness to Japanese men—who leave their families at 7 a.m., commute long distances, and return at 11 p.m., having been drinking after hours with their officemates to "get to know each other better"— it is hard to maintain any semblance of family life. Men's focus is primarily on the company. If given free time, the majority of men prefer to play golf (the status game) than to stay at home. In consequence, when the men retire, they are called *sodai-gomi*, big garbage, or *nure-ochiba*, clinging wet leaf, because they usually have developed few, if any, hobbies or interests and, so, stay at home. Divorce rates are high among retired men and their wives, who have become accustomed to living independently.

The inevitable questions arose among the women, such as if women are expected to stay at home and raise the children, what kind of fulfillment do they find after their youngest child goes off to college, or is married? Also, in the United States and in Japan, the fastest growing segment of the population is the old-old group, those over 85 years old, mostly women. If a woman's youngest child leaves home by the time the mother is 55 years old, what will the next 30 years bring?

No society is perfect, but I think American women have far more opportunities that most women in other countries.

Sincerely,

Joan Mondale

January, 1996
A Typical Week

Some of you are probably wondering just what does the wife of the American ambassador do, besides entertain? Here is a typical week in my life:

Sunday, Nov. 12   6:00 a.m.   Earthquake tremors.

I spent all day at my desk, organizing for the coming week.

Monday, Nov. 13   9:30 a.m.   A car and driver picked me up to go to the Tokyo Chamber of Commerce and Industry to speak to their Business Women's Club. The topic was "Today's Woman: Options, Role Models, and Success Stories." The members were presidents of small businesses; they were not activists. After the questions and answers, they presented me with a scarf, designed and produced by one of their companies, and a slab- built, blue and green *oribe* platter, mounted on a low, thrown pedestal.

noon   After a quick bowl of soup at the residence, where I spotted twelve newly returned azure-winged magpies flying around the garden, I asked Fritz's driver to take me to pick up the dry cleaning. The usually short trip took an hour, because the traffic was so slow.

January, 1996 *A Typical Week*

6:00 p.m.   At the Tokyo American Club, I accepted a Distinguished Achievement Award on behalf of Haru Reischauer, widow of the late Ambassador Edwin O. Reischauer, my father's first cousin. Haru was unable tocome to Japan, so she sent her message to me by fax. Four others were honored: Jean Pearce, a journalist with *The Japan Times*, who has been writing a column called "Getting Things Done" for thirty years; Dr. Donald Keene, author, editor, and teacher of Japanese literature; Dr. Leo Esaki, winner of the Nobel Laureate in physics for developing the tunnel semiconductor diode; and Tetsuko Kuroyanagi, host of a daily talk show, actress, and goodwill ambassador for UNICEF. Her well-known book, *Totto-chan, the Little Girl at theWindow*, was one of the first books recommended to me to read before coming to Japan.

Four of the winners line up to have their pictures taken. From left to right: Jean Pearce, Dr. Donald Keene, Dr. Leo Esaki, and Tetsuko Kuroyanagi.

Tuesday, Nov. 14

9:00 a.m. Kay Brennan picked me up to take a trip to China Pete's, a porcelain and pottery outlet store about two hours away, near the army base Camp Zama in Sagamihara. I had always heard about it, but never had the chance to go there. I bought some Christmas presents for Lynda Pedersen, Fritz's terrific secretary. Her husband, Paul, who urged her to come to Japan with us, owns and operates the Gray's Bay Marina in Wayzata, so fish motifs are always appreciated. I bought five *hashi-okis* (chopstick holders) in the shape of four fish and an octopus. Our chef supplied the names of the fish.

5:00 p.m. We returned to Tokyo in time to dress for a farewell dinner at the Norwegian Embassy in honor of Kunihiko Saito, the newly appointed Japanese ambassador to the United States, and his wife, Akiko. They are eagerly waiting for the assignment to begin and they will be excellent representatives of Japan. Before dinner our hostess Ellen Bjorneby played her flute in a duet with a Japanese female *koto* player. They had hoped that the Norwegian author Jostein Gaarder, who wrote *Sophie's World*, would attend. He was unable to, but each of the guests received an autographed copy of his book. Fritz was surprised to see that Gaarder had once worked in the Hotel Mundal, owned by Fritz's relatives in Mundal, on the Fjaerland fjord.

Wednesday, Nov. 15

7:30 a.m. WCCO-TV arrived on our doorstep to film Fritz and me at breakfast. Then, down the hill to the Embassy for photoshots in the office, and back up the hill to

January 1996 *A Typical Week*

film Minneapolis Mayor Sharon Sayles Belton and a group from the Greater Minneapolis Convention and Visitors Association, including Eiji Oue, music director of the Minnesota Orchestra, and David Hyslop, president of the Orchestral Association, and his wife, Sally.

I then took the WCCO-TV crew to the Meiji Shrine to see *Shichi-go-san*. Children ages three, five, and seven are dressed in traditional kimonos and taken by their parents and grandparents to the shrine to celebrate the custom of praying for the children's safe and healthy futures.

We sped off to see *The Seven Lucky Gods*, a bronze figurative and narrative work by Minneapolis sculptor Douglas Freeman. The seven gods are called *Shichifukujin*. and in former

- **A mother and daughter rest a moment before going into the shrine on Shichi-go-san day.**

times people tucked woodblock prints of them under their pillows on New Years' to bring good fortune. The figures were commissioned as public art for the plaza connecting three new buildings at the Akabane train station in north Tokyo. I had helped dedicate them earlier in the month. Mr. Yanagihara, president of the project's architectural firm, visited Douglas Freeman in his south Minneapolis studio, where the sculptor modeled a portrait of Mr. Yanagihara as the Chinese Zen priest, Hotei. The resemblance was remarkable!

7:00 p.m.   Dinner at the International House, in Roppongi, a twenty-minute walk from our residence. "I House" is an inn which the Rockefeller brothers built for visiting scholars. Right now, for example, Kitty Eisele, who won an Academy Award for choosing the still photographs for the PBS Civil War Series, is staying there. She was given a fellowship by the Japan Society to study Japanese women at work, and historic preservation. Jack Lenor Larsen, the renowned textile designer, came to town and invited me, Reiko Sudo (the main designer for Nuno, a shop for contemporary textiles), and Hisako Sekijima, a basket artist, for an informal gathering.

Thursday, Nov. 16

9:00 a.m.   The Asian Pacific Economic Cooperation meeting is approaching and we need to prepare for the president's arrival. Miyako Kato, Residence Manager; John Wascoat, a steward from Montana; and I took the van to Yokosuka Navy base to shop for the "wheels up" party for the Clinton advance team, many of whom had advanced for us in 1984. Just as I was piling lettuce into my grocery cart, the call came that President Clinton was not coming to APEC in Osaka, nor to Tokyo for a visit with the emperor and empress and Prime Minister Murayama. Everything was cancelled. I was so sad to have to put the lettuce back! Later, I wrote Hillary Clinton a note saying how sorry we were that they couldn't come, but at least her proposed visit prompted the officials of the public art at Shinjuku i-Land to replenish the water in the fountain, which forms an integral part of one of the marble sculptures.

6:00 p.m. After returning from the long drive, I hopped into party clothes for a dinner to celebrate the artist Roy Lichtenstein's winning of the coveted Kyoto Prize.

Friday, Nov. 17

9-6 p.m. This was another day at my desk, answering mail and writing this article for the *Hill & Lake Press*.

Sincerely,

Joan Mondale

February, 1996
Lunch with Their Majesties

One sunny day we were invited to have lunch with Emperor Akihito and Empress Michiko-sama (*sama* is a very polite honorific). We joined three other ambassadors and their wives: Amos and Dala Ganor from Israel; José Ramon Sanchis Muñoz and his wife, Polly Ferman, from Argentina; and Wu Dawei and Wang Yueqin from China. A little over two years ago, the four couples came to a reception honoring those of us who were new arrivals.

We drove through the Sakashita-mon Gate toward the north porch of the Palace. Once inside the Imperial grounds, it seems as though you are in another world. Tokyo is busy, restless, crowded, and very urban. The palace buildings are set in a vast, unpopulated forest. The main building is a huge one-story, Japanese-style building, with long, wide passages carpeted in deep yellow. The sixteen-petaled chrysanthemun, symbol of royalty, is found everywhere. After walking for what seemed like an eternity, we were escorted into an empty room. We whispered among ourselves, reminding each other that we were not allowed to extend our hand to shake hands first, nor could we speak first. A great hush fell over the group when the ladies-in-waiting slipped into the room, for we could sense that the Imperial family was about to enter. They did, with hands outstretched and pleasant greetings on their lips. The emperor wore a business suit and the empress wore a pale pink kimono. We returned their greetings with, "Your Majesty." When we addressed a member of the family, we said, "Your Royal Highness." However, we were not required to curtsey. (Christina Valquist from Sweden and Renate von Nouhuys from The Netherlands had told me that they were comfortable with royalty and curtsey instinctively.)

The luncheon was a gourmet treat! The menu was: *consommé chatelaine*, *amadai au safran*, *noisette de mouton rotie*, *salade de saison*, *marrons chantilly*, and dessert. I was seated next to Prince Akishino, the emperor's second son. Crown Prince Naruhito, who married American-educated Masako, is more familiar to us. Fritz sat next to Princess Akishino, whose first name is Kiko. Polly Ferman, who was seated across the table, was skillful in asking leading questions to keep the conversation going. Throughout the luncheon, we heard an orchestra playing music, representative of each of our nations.

We said good-bye to our hosts, then followed them down the long corridors as we walked out. We signed the guest book and joined our drivers, who were waiting to return us to the real world.

Sincerely,

Joan Mondale

March, 1996
The Cost of Living

Japan is the most expensive country in the world. That is easily said, but what does it mean to those Americans who live here, serving our country? One can of Campbell's soup bought in Japan costs five times as much as the same can bought in the United States. The price of a box of cold cereal costs four times as much as an identical box on the shelves of American grocery stores. A friend visiting Japan dropped into a camera shop to buy a lens cover. She saw a Nikon lens priced at $395. It was the same as the lens for which she paid $150 in Minneapolis.

Ed Lincoln, a noted economist on loan to us from the Brookings Institution, and his wife conducted a cost comparison with a friend in the States of food prices on the same day in Tokyo and in Washington, D.C. The results were astonishing.

March, 1996 *The Cost of Living*

Price Comparison Between Tokyo and Washington
December 13/15, 1995
Prices in U.S. Dollars (Assume $1.00 = ¥100)

Item	Unit	Meidi-ya Tokyo	Giant Foods Washington
Apples	907 grams	5.80	$ 1.76
Grapefruit	one	5.00	$ 0.66
Lettuce	one	3.32	$ 0.64
Potatoes	500 grams	4.04	$ 1.08
Tomatoes	400 grams	4.50	$ 1.76
Chicken Breast	400 grams	10.87	$ 2.20
Ground Beef	200 grams	9.32	$ 0.88
Milk	1 liter	2.15	$ 0.90
Margarine	225 grams	1.95	$ 0.39
Bread	200 grams	3.00	$ 0.26
Coca-Cola	1.5 liters	3.20	$ 0.66
Cod	200 grams	5.00	$ 2.42
TOTAL (excluding tax)		**$58.15**	**$13.61**

Conversion Chart

1 gram= .0353 ounces	1 ounce = 28.35 grams
1 liter =1.0571 quarts	1 quart = .946 liters

What costs $58.15 in Tokyo would cost $13.61 in Washington.

The Lincolns conducted interviews with Americans in Tokyo, asking them how the high cost of living affected their lives. Their answers were similiar. One person said, "Instead of attending events at the Kennedy Center, going to one or two movies a week, eating out at good restaurants and frequently traveling, our entertainment here consists mainly of watching videos at home, eating out at 'cheap eats' (at a cost of twenty to thirty dollars per person, no drinks) and walking around Tokyo. The lifestyle here compared with in the United States is enormously constrained and constricted." Another person said, "We have been to a restaurant as a family once in the past year. With movies costing eighteen dollars without food or transportation, we cannot even go to the movies. No dinners out. No movies. No theater or concerts. No travel. No shopping."

One career officer for our Embassy said, "In my past assignments, I have explored the country—to learn about the culture and make-up of the country and, most important, to get to know the people, to understand their background, and current concerns. I consider this to be part of my job as an American diplomat. Traveling in Japan is prohibitive. Instead of getting to know this country and its people, I find myself moving between the embassy, the compound [where embassy staff and their families live], and the New Sanno Hotel [a military hotel with shops and restaurants]."

Our country is blessed by superb career officers who serve our nation around the world, along with their families. They are prepared to sacrifice, but the cruel cost squeeze in Japan goes beyond what we should ask them to suffer on our behalf. They are the best and they deserve our appreciation and support.

Sincerely,

Joan Mondale

April, 1996
Kindling the Home Fires

A LETTER FROM AMY KATOH

Amy Katoh is an American who founded The Blue and White shop twenty years ago in the Azabujuban section of Tokyo. She scouts the countryside for artists who use traditional indigo and white designs. She commissions them to make contemporary work for her shop. In essence, she is helping the Japanese appreciate their own craft traditions.

Amy wrote this article as a thank you for dinner at our residence before a roaring fire.

When I missed the great tree pruning at Arisugawa Park, I also missed my chance for free firewood this year, but I was prepared to pay the price, I thought.

Over recent years I have noticed— how could you miss it?—the levelling of all those rickety wooden buildings that once gave Tokyo its character. The vegetable shop, the tofu man, the barber, the pickle shops have been quietly disappearing, torn down and replaced with abysmal blocks of bathroom-tiled "mansions." I have watched it happen, and mourned the passing of traditional Japanese neighborhood architecture, the sinewy grey roof tiles, the plaster, the weather-worn wood, the plantings, the blooms of each seasons. I have cried when I have seen the tasteless replacements, the pseudo-brick veneer sidings, the burnished

Amy Katoh, married to Yuichi and mother of four children, serves as a focal point for the American community. She is everywhere, a creative spirit.

bronze-like relief doors, the prefabricated jerry-built houses that have come to replace the carpenters' handbuilt works made from natural materials and human effort. Classic monuments of Japanese taste and Japanese skill and in some cases pure Japanese perserverence. After fires, after earthquakes and other calamities, the instinct was to get something up, anything would do, a roof over the head for work and living, often in that order. So while what was there was not often beautiful, it was Japanese, built by hammer and saw, and often environmentally ahead of the times, with a bow to the season tree here, a window box of flowers there, and a little earth at the fringes—ask any dog! They were messy sometimes, and there was a certain dishevelment to some, but they were on a human scale and made of real materials. And they answered all the needs of life. Communities acted and interacted harmoniously within and among their walls. Things worked and people worked and were happy, though life wasn't always easy, and mod conveniences were not had by all. Then they started to be introduced in large cold geometric blocks of bathroomlike tiles of all shades and sizes, with fussy fluted balconies and upscale names like Stately Homes, Green Hills Aoyama, Minami Azabu Mansion. Slowly, silently the wooden shacks have all disappeared and with them, unnoticed, a whole way of life has also vanished—poof!

Try to find firewood in Tokyo now! It used to be a necessity of life. Now it is the greatest of luxuries to find fuel for a fire for one of Tokyo's few snowy nights. I found this out recently when I combed the old shops that used to sell firewood and charcoal. Now you can hardly find them either; most of the shops are gone. I went to Murata's, the old place that we have been using for twenty years. It has been rebuilt, tiled, and is spic and span, not a trace of kindling or charcoal or commerce of any kind. "He died five years ago, and we stopped selling firewood then. But when he was alive, we did a thriving business all right," said his sharp-witted wife, an old lady now with blackened hair and a rounded back which clearly gave her pain. She recalled the old days with fondness.

Was there any other place she knew about nearby? I asked. She told me of several other places in Azabu. "Nope, that one's gone. No, they don't sell wood anymore," I answered, having already investigated myself. "Isn't there anywhere else?" I asked, desperate by now. "Well, there is Furukawa-kan, over by Shin no Hashi" [that means new bridge, though it's not exactly new, having been built and so named in 1870 or so, during the Meiji Era]. "I'll call him." And the call went on for a good twenty minutes. "How are you? It's been a long time. Thanks to you I am fine. Thank you for the other day. Not the same since he died. How busy we were. Remember when . . ." and on and on. Here obviously were two old friends who had been through many things together. The conversation went on and on. Just as I thought they were getting to the point, they would drift off to another memory. The hour was drawing late. Twelve people were coming for dinner that night, I had yet to set the table, and the firewood wasn't even a possibility so far. The cozy fire I had envisioned hung in the balance of this rambling conversation between two old friends. They clearly hadn't spoken in years and had lots to catch up on. At the other end of the line from my old *obaachan* was my last hope for firewood. "And remember how busy it was in the old days? A little snow like this and they'd be lined up. What good times they were! He worked hard and he loved it! He'd load up that truck and go around delivering. It was a lot of work. Oh no? Too bad! Well maybe?" Enough of these memories! Did they have the firewood or not? But who was she talking to? Let them keep talking if only I could figure how to find the person on the other end of the line. The directions took another 15 minutes, and the thanks and leave taking another 10, though getting there was easy. Furukawa-kan was a quick drive, a modern, tiled building if you will, with a roll-up shutter. And there, sitting out in front, was gold! Four neat bundles of firewood. A bright-looking young man was busily moving about his work, and scuffling about on his own business was a slightly bent but spritely old man with a head of white hair topped with a handknit cap. He had on a flannel shirt and a sleeveless sweater. His eyes still sparkled with the pleasure of that phone call. He was delighted to have the firewood. He was the epitome of the hundreds of *ojiisan* I have bantered with and cajoled in my years in Japan. It has always been those twinkling and good-hearted resourceful *ojiisan* who have answered my prayers. This man embodied that magic power of old Japan in which it seemed anything could be done: people, would work and work and make the impossible happen. Never mind that the bundle of firewood, four fairly small pieces, cost ¥1,000 (ten dollars)! That was beside the point at this hour. He had it and I had found him. I brought it home, rejoicing.

The party was lovely and I was ready when the guests arrived, but the floor heating generated ample heat and the fire seemed somewhat superfluous. My efforts were totally invisible. No more fires, I thought. You really don't need them in this day and age. Or so I thought until the next night when we were invited by the Mondales to a very special evening at the American Embassy Residence. It was a beautiful night filled with snow. We walked into the great room, where the guests were already gathered around a roaring fire four or five massive logs high. The fire was blazed and reflected off the brass andirons in the beautifully restored fireplace. Conversation crackled and spirits sparked in front of the fire. It was the all-time classic fire and I was disappointed when we were called in for dinner. The fire was going beautifully and I hated to leave it. When I remarked on this to our gracious host, he said enthusiastically, "Don't worry. We've got another one in the dining room!" My eyes popped in wonder. How ever had they gotten so much firewood in this city where I had spent days in search of four bundles? I had to ask. "It's American. It's cheaper that way," the ambassador exclaimed with his own glow. We feasted in front of a crackling fire in a magic room of happy friendship.

Sincerely,

Amy Katoh

May, 1996
Those Ubiquitous Cherry Blossoms

Cherry blossoms and Japan are synonymous. References to *sakura* (cherry blossoms) abound in Japanese life and are deeply embedded in the national consciousness. As a symbol of renewal and spring, the cherry blossoms are welcomed with deep emotions, for they are reminders of how beautiful, but how short, life is. They burst into bloom and just as quickly fall like snowflakes, covering the ground with their soft, pale pink petals. People are happy just to sit and look at them and cherry blossom-viewing parties, *ohanami*, are quickly organized. (The youngest members of the company are dispatched at dawn to stake out a space, usually in a cemetery, to save it for compatriots who arrive with picnic lunches, *obento*, and bottles of sake.) The saying goes, "Under the cherry blossoms, we all become friends."

Sakura imagery permeates the arts; it appears in haiku poetry, in patterns on kimonos, as the subject of scroll paintings, and as designs on lacquer boxes, chopstick holders (*hashi-oki*) and sword guards. Names of streets, banks, and even announcements of the results of university entrance exams are coined in *sakura* language. *Sakura saku* means acceptance and *sakura chiru* means failure.

May, 1996   *Those Ubiquitous Cherry Blossoms*

•

Fritz took many pictures of Haru Reischauer's cherry tree in bloom to send to her in San Diego, where she lives now. The Okura Hotel is seen in the background.

•

This pink dogwood will be the only reminder of our stay in Japan. It will long outlive us! The three bamboo stakes help support the young tree.

Many famous haiku poems refer to cherry blossoms.

Evening cherry blossoms	Talking stops—	Through petals
Today also now belongs	white petals	on the pond,
To the past.	falling in my heart.	eye of the frog.
ISSA	TAKEO	FUSEI

111

Around mid-March, newspapers carry daily announcements about the blossoms' appearance in Kyushu (the southernmost island). By the first of April, they suddenly appear on the scene in Tokyo, with no warning, for there are no green leaves to herald their coming—the leaves come out at the same time as the blossoms. They signal the start of the school year and the hiring of new employees in businesses.

In ancient times, cherry blossom viewing was not just a diversion, it was a fortune-telling ritual. If the blossoms came out in profusion, crops would thrive and the harvest would be plentiful. Cherry trees were thought to be companions of the gods, *kami*, who lived in a lofty, heavenly realm, and who were believed to enter and exit the world of man by passing through the trees.

We have several cherry trees in our garden, planted by wives of American ambassadors. Mrs. Joseph C. Grew planted one in 1942 when the staff was under house arrest during World War II, and Mrs. Edwin O. Reischauer (Haru) planted hers in 1966. The tree I planted was a pink dogwood, and, I am glad to say, it is doing well.

Sincerely,

Joan Mondale

P.S. By 5 p.m. on Saturday, April 6, an estimated 96,900 people had visited Ueno Park in Tokyo, a popular place for ohanami.

June, 1996
The Clintons Come to Visit

Helicopters, motorcades, twenty-two thousand police on duty, and two airplanes of Americans interrupted the throbbing pace of life in Tokyo. We stood on the tarmac in the pouring rain, waiting to welcome President Bill Clinton and Hillary, Secretary of State Warren Christopher, and other administration officials for a state visit to Japan, April 16–18. When the 747 came into view, I must admit I felt very homesick to see "The United States of America" emblazoned on a blue background the entire length of the plane. We heard the 21-gun salute in the distance as the President and First Lady de-

Prime Minister Ryutaro Hashimoto presented President Bill Clinton with a baseball glove at the private dinner in the Akasaka Guest House. Akiko Saito and Kumiko Hashimoto are seated on either side of the President.

- Carp, or *koi*, are considered as the "king of the river fish".

scended the stairs from the plane. (The press plane followed without ceremony.)

The two-and-a-half day visit began quietly that evening, with a small, private dinner with Prime Minister Ryutaro Hashimoto and his wife, Kumiko; Ambassador to the United States Kunihiko Saito and his wife, Akiko; the Clintons; and Fritz and me at the Akasaka Guest House annex, on the Akasaka Guest House grounds, where the Clintons were staying. Our Japanese meal was served by the kimono-clad staff from the famous Tokyo restaurant, Kitcho. Hashimoto was clearly energized by his important guest of honor and talked enthusiastically throughout the dinner. The president and the prime minister seemed to have a very good personal relationship. We fed the carp from the balcony. They were black, gray, white, yellow, and orange, swarming on top of each other to reach the dry pellets of food we tossed to them. Carp are greatly valued in Japan and some have been known to live as long as 50 years. They symbolize strength and courage and are traditionally depicted on the kimonos worn by boys on Boy's Day, May 5. They are also the inspiration for the flying carp streamers.

June, 1996 *The Clintons Come to Visit*

The next day dawned bright and clear. After the Imperial family welcomed the Clintons at the Akasaka Guest House, we all went to the Imperial Palace for the state call. The high point of the visit for me was the luncheon at our residence for Hillary Clinton to meet thirteen Japanese career women. I toasted her by saying, "Welcome to our residence. I am so glad you could come for lunch. We are honored and happy to have all of you. As we have looked forward to the coming of the cherry blossoms, so we have looked forward to your visit. We know that you care deeply about women's rights, which, after all, are basic human rights—your speech in Beijing still resonates. We want to strengthen the friendship, understanding, appreciation, and respect between our two great nations. So, today, we have invited women who have excelled in their fields to talk about women in Japan. We are grateful for all you are doing for our country. Will you join me as we raise our glasses in honor of Hillary Clinton. Kampai!" She responded by saying women throughout the world have much more in common than that which separates them. During lunch, she asked each guest's name and what she hoped to accomplish. One of the most revealing comments was made by Kaori Sasaki, who runs a support group for female executives, who said that the reason there was almost no networking here was that students are told to accept what is taught and they are not taught to share. Hiroko Kuniya, who has a daily news program on television, said she wanted to inform the public about issues, so she could encourage debate, since there is little, if any, in Japan. I thought Hillary captured the imagination of many women in a country where women's career options are

LETTERS FROM JAPAN

First Lady Hillary Rodham Clinton raises a glass as I offer a toast during the luncheon in her honor. I invited women prominent in their fields to talk about the position of women in Japan. To Mrs. Clinton's left is Professor Asako Notoji.

sharply limited. For most, the idea of combining a career and a high-profile public role with marriage and motherhood is hard to even imagine. Mariko Bando, a prefectural vice governor, said later, "She was very energetic; I was impressed by her intelligence and the way she says things so frankly. She listened to each of us carefully and replied with frank comments—not as the president's wife, but as an individual woman who has a career." The luncheon menu was Japanese spring salad, tomato cream soup, asparagus salad with orange mousse and assorted fruit for dessert. The table was decorated with freshly cut branches of pink cherry blossoms. Hillary and I left the luncheon and the press descended upon the guests like locusts. We took helicopters with our husbands to Yokosuka Naval

June, 1996 *The Clintons Come to Visit*

Base to greet thousands of military personnel and their families on the deck of the aircraft carrier, U.S.S. *Independence*. Its flag, "Don't Tread on Me," has always flown on the oldest naval vessel in service since the American Revolutionary War. (The "Indy" requires a crew of five thousand.)

That night we attended an elegant white tie banquet at the Imperial Palace. I sat next to the powerful cabinet secretary Seiroku Kajiyama, who, in a very untypical way, made me laugh so hard I almost couldn't eat. His views about women were reminiscent of the 1950s in the United States and I think he was sincere when he told me that a woman's place was in the home.

On Thursday, April 18, President Clinton addressed a joint session of the Diet, the Japanese parliament. The speech was well-received and was warmly applauded. Then the President and First Lady greeted members of our Embassy staff and their families at our residence. (Hillary told us about the time the motorcade left Chelsea behind and she had to hop into the follow-up car with all the baggage.)

Fritz and I drove in yet another motorcade to Haneda Airport to wave good-bye, relieved that it had been a successful visit. I believe the Japanese were very pleased with the state visit, as were we. So were our guests at the "wheels up" party that night. We also invited the Japanese counterparts to our American advance team. Everyone was having such a good time that we had to dim the lights to get them to go home!

Sincerely,

Joan Mondale

July, 1996

Japanese Ghosts

In Tokyo, as in Washington, D.C., there is an abundance of famous visitors, seen and unseen. I was invited to an elegant luncheon in honor of Mrs. Boutros Boutros-Ghali, wife of the secretary general of the United Nations. It was hosted by Mrs. Heitor Gurgulino de Souza, wife of the rector of the United Nations University in Tokyo. (Our own Harlan Cleveland, former head of the Humphrey Institute at the University of Minnesota, will be teaching at the Institute for Advanced Studies there next year.) Mrs. Boutros-Ghali told me that she had grown up in Alexandria and a mutual friend introduced her to her future husband, who lived in Cairo. Theirs was a long-distance romance. She brought her husband's best wishes to Fritz, who had worked with him in 1979 on the peace process between Egypt and Israel that resulted in the Camp David accords. She spoke passionately about the erosion of women's rights by the fundamentalists in Egypt.

The luncheon guest list read like a Who's Who of Tokyo. Sitting across from me was Yumiko Owada, whose husband represents Japan at the United Nations and who is the mother of Princess Masako, the wife of the crown prince. To my left was Chako Hatakeyama, director of the Hatakeyama Collection (tea utensils, etc.) and vice chairman of the Worldwide Fund for

Nature–Japan. Mrs. Maria Reis, wife of the ambassador from Brazil, joined our conversation. She looked slightly harried and wondered out loud why she felt more tired in Tokyo than she had ever felt in other capital cities where she had lived. I have often heard that comment from others. I could give no explanation, except that Tokyo is never still, with so much going on. (I had just come back from a visit to Sezon Museum, six miles away, to see a Noguchi/Rosanjin exhibition. The round trip took three hours!)

Unaccountably, the conversation turned to the telling of ghost stories. Chako Hatakeyama recounted "Ban-cho Sara Yashiki" (*Ban-cho* is the name of an old town, *sara* means plate, and *yashiki* is a samurai's house). It is a famous legend of a maid who was accused of breaking the tenth plate of a set. Her master pushed her down a well and from that time on, her voice could be heard, counting the plates. When she reached the number ten, a loud scream would emerge from the well. Chako also told a true story of a friend who visited the home of an old friend. As she entered the house, the beloved, elderly maid bowed to her in greeting. Later, she remarked that the maid certainly must be rather old by now, because she remembered the maid from her childhood. Her hostess recoiled in horror and said that the maid had died three months ago.

I told my ghost story. Three days after our dog Digger had died, I distinctly heard the jingle of the tags on her collar, as if she were coming down the stairs behind me. I stopped and looked around, but, of course, there was no Digger.

As of yet, no ghosts have appeared in our residence. We've been looking for General Douglas MacArthur, but he has not been seen. However, we finally found the tombstone for his cat, Pinky Purr.

Sincerely,

Joan Mondale

- **A Kabuki actor in full costume.**

August, 1996
America's Birthday, Tokyo Style

The height of activity for our staff is the preparation for our July 4 celebration. One thousand people are invited, in two shifts. Elected and government officials, the military, and ambassadors come in the morning. (This year, we were pleased that Prime Minister Hashimoto came. Fritz and he met privately in the library.) Everyone else comes in the afternoon—friends, artists, neighbors, and many in the American community, along with senior embassy staff and their spouses.

We put up long, white tents out-of-doors, since June and July are the rainy season and last summer it poured. We put American flags all over the garden with long banners and bunting decorating the front entrance. We barbequed hot dogs and hamburgers by the pool, which the pool man had been cleaning every day for two weeks. The resident manager, Miyako Kato, and I had made the hour-and-a-half-long trip to the commissary at Yokota Air Force base to buy the food, including 80 pounds of hamburger! (This year we didn't serve spare ribs, and lots of guests asked for them, so back they go on the menu.)

Fortunately, the sun shone and all the guests wore their best clothes and big smiles, especially when they ate chocolate-covered ice cream, a welcome donation from Mike Sullivan, president of Minnesota-based Dairy Queen. I thought the Dairy Queen logo, emblazoned on the ice chests, symbolized America and home. Five members of the military band from Yokosuka Naval base played American music, chosen to appeal to all tastes.

Everything went smoothly. The Okura Hotel let us use their parking lot across the street. Our staff of ten was not adequate to serve that many guests, so Mrs. Kato hired waiters, waitresses, and cooks (all of whom were friends of our staff) from three hotels nearby.

Fritz and I shook everyone's hand and smiled broadly for the never-ending picture taking sessions. Many ambassadors wore their national

•

Prime Minister Hashimoto stopped by our 4th of July celebration. He brought his interpreter with him. Fritz and he met in our library, where General Douglas MacArthur loved to listen to music and where Ambassador Joseph C. Grew had his private office in the 1930's.

The Imaizumi Imaemon XIII Arita's porcelain pot, presented to the residence by the Obyashi construction company, sits on the coffee table. The books of my fledgling collection by or about U.S. Ambassadors are tucked on the shelf behind earthquake-proof grilled doors.

August, 1996 *America's Birthday, Tokyo Style*

Noraneko eating his supper.

dress. Those from African nations outshone everyone. But both the United States and Japanese military officers wore striking white summer uniforms with lots of gold braid and medals.

The only tragedy of the day was that our stray cat, Noraneko (*nora* means wild and *neko* means cat), temporarily lost his house, due to inattentive workmen who put up the tents. He made a brief appearance, then slipped away for some peace and quiet, and anonymity, somewhere else. After the last guest left, we put his house back together again and gave him a special dinner, served by Fritz's uniformed waiter, who carried fresh water for Noraneko in a silver pitcher.

Because the event is so big, we rely on the cooperation of the Akasaka police to direct traffic. It was a thrilling sight to see the diplomatic cars driving up to the front door with their nation's flags flying. Afterward, we took food to the police headquarters to show our gratitude. Mrs. Kato distributed the many flowers to all our helpers.

One of our guests, Bill Hersey, an American expatriate, wrote a thank-you note saying that the guests, decorations, music and the food all added up to a very memorable event. He wrote, "I want to say I was proud to be an American." And so are we!

Sincerely,

Joan Mondale

September, 1996
A Visit to Yokosuka and American Students in Japan

One Saturday, the vice admiral of the Seventh Fleet gave a reception for us on board the USS *Blue Ridge*, the command vessel for the entire fleet in the Pacific Ocean. We flew by helicopter from Hardy Barracks in Tokyo to Yokosuka Naval base and were immediately officially piped on board. The reception served as a goodwill gesture to the Japanese, for half of the guests were dignitaries and citizens of the town of Yokosuka. The mayor presented me with a *kutani* pot; its shape showed that the potter was influenced by Persian ceramics and the decoration depicted figures from Chinese mythology. It came in its own special wooden box made of *kiri* wood, sturdy and fire-resistant.

Flags were flying everywhere and the Minnesota State Office lent the admiral our state flag. Fritz opened his remarks by pointing out the flags of three great nations: the United States, Japan, and Minnesota! We met several Minnesotans in the receiving line and then we all posed for the mandatory photograph on the upper deck. There were fourteen of us. Among them were Lynda Pedersen, Fritz's administrative secretary from Wayzata, Lt. Joy Hopkins from Red Wing, Capt. J.P. Brusseau of Buffalo Lake, Col. and Mrs. Bill Wesley of Minneapolis, Capt. Mark Lenci of Virginia, and Blake Longacre from Minneapolis, who joined us from

September, 1996 *A Visit to Yokosuka*

Kanagawa, where he's part of a Youth for Understanding short-term study program. He is living with a Japanese family and playing basketball. He finds that learning the Japanese language is fun!

The State Department has a summer internship program. Angie Ray, from Bone Lake of Scandia, Minnesota, is working in the Environment, Science, and Technology section of our embassy until she returns to Nanzan University in Nagoya in the fall. There she will be a senior, completing a double major in the Japanese language and international relations. Her minor is international business. (She started learning Japanese when she was a freshman in college. She found it so compelling that she has continued studying it.)

One of Fritz's goals is to encourage more Americans to come to Japan to study. Over forty-seven thousand Japanese are studying in our colleges and universities, while only thirteen hundred Americans are enrolled in Japan's schools. There are many reasons for this: the high cost of living, the language barrier, and other restrictions.

Earlier this year, Fritz received a group of fifteen high school students from the Minneapolis Public Schools who were studying the Japanese language. Their three teachers accompanied them. Fritz asked them why they had decided to study Japanese and many of them said because it was a challenge, and because it was so different from English.

Because the fastest-growing, dynamic

economies are to be found in Asia, Fritz spoke to them about how important it is for us to learn, understand, and appreciate Japan, as it has been for the Japanese to understand us. He spoke of how they are proud of their culture and consider it the best, just as we think America is the best! Those high school students will have an experience that no one can take away—a curiosity and zest for learning that will be theirs for the rest of their lives. We hope to have many more students learning Japanese. This program in the Minneapolis Public Schools certainly deserves our support.

Sincerely,

Joan Mondale

- **We were happy to greet all the Minnesotans aboard the USS Blue Ridge. They reminded us of home. Lynda Pedersen, to our left, is Fritz's Administrative Assistant.**

October, 1996
Marriage and Art in Public Places

Ambassadors' wives have many roles to fill. The first and foremost is to serve as the hostess for official entertaining, which never seems to cease! In addition to that, I sought to keep up my interest in the arts, including pottery and ceramics. In deciding what to emphasize, I asked Art Zegelbone, our cultural attaché to help me by inviting some Japanese professionals from the art world for lunch to see if we could create a proper role for me. We agreed that since the idea of art in public places was just beginning to take hold in Japan that I could be an advocate for public art, an audience-builder, educator, and cheerleader. So we wrote a speech, collected slides of American public art, and bought a video, *Arts-on-the-Line*, a prize-winning film about art on the Red Line extension of the Boston subway system.

I have given that speech many times, altering it as I go along. Now that the art world knows what special area of art I care a lot about, I have been invited to celebrations dedicating public art throughout Japan. At Akebane Station Plaza, I was pleased to meet Douglas Freeman, a sculptor from Minneapolis who was commissioned to create *Shichifukujin*, or Seven Lucky Gods, in bronze. He was chosen because the Japanese architectural firm wanted the figurative and narrative work to have a fresh interpre-

• Love blossomed into two spring weddings. Masami Ichida, chef of the DCM residence, married Sachiko ("Chako") from our staff. They had met in our kitchen. The ceremony took place in our residence. The reception afterwards was held in the dining room, which was turned into a garden. Branches of cherry trees were flown in from Izu to bloom on their wedding day.

• Our faithful steward, Imre Hegedus, is a Hungarian who immigrated to Japan, following Etsuko, whom he met in Budapest. They were married at the Hikawa shrine. Imre's friends from the Hungarian embassy prepared delicious food with lots of paprika.

tation, knowing a Japanese artist would most likely render the figures in the traditional manner. A good example was the figure of Ebisu, who usually carries a fish tucked under his arm. Douglas Freeman depicted Ebisu running after the fish, holding tightly onto its tail. Traditionally, the fish has been a seabream. Since Freeman had never encountered one before, he ordered a fresh one from Coastal Seafoods, so he could make a model from life. Imagine his surprise when he came to pick up the fish to find it had been turned into filets! A search through the garbage can yielded the head for his inspection.

October, 1996 *Marriage and Art in Public Places*

•
Ebisu runs after the fish, with his fishing pole curved around his back.

•
Robert Indiana's "Love" is becoming the symbol of Shinjuku i-Land, a project Fumio Nanjo, public art consultant, has put together for the Housing and Urban Development Corporation. He chose a few artists to create large pieces. Fritz and his guard, Mizuta, walk toward the famous sculpture.

•
Claes Oldenburg and Coosje van Bruggen came to dinner one evening with their daughter. I invited Li Lundin, who writes reviews of art exhibits in Japan for a Chinese magazine in Taipei. She is married to a USIS staffer. We went to many shows together. Fumio Nanjo, to my left, enjoys a conversation with Claes Oldenburg.

129

The Housing and Urban Development Corporation (HUDC), a public/private organization in Japan, has been instrumental in using a percent for art from the construction budget in two spectacular complexes: Shinjuku i-Land and Faret Tachikawa. In the video HUDC officials gave me to include in my talk, artists from all over the world speak about their installations, including Roy Lichtenstein, Stephen Antonakos, and Joseph Kosuth. Now I have added a third video from Minnesota, *The Green Chair Project*, which was originated by Minneapolis sculptor Joel Sisson, a recent graduate of the Minneapolis College of Art and Design. He used his critical vision to fill a social need by cooperating with neighborhood teenagers in the production of public art: wooden Adirondack chairs, painted a

- **Faret Tachikawa is a huge development project on the site of an American World War II air base. Fram Kitagawa, a public art consultant, chose artists from Japan and abroad to create commissioned works of art to be incorporated into the development. We are sitting on a Niki de Saint Phalle double chair, preparing for a press interview.**

uniform green. (I'm sure you have seen their giant counterparts around town.)

I'm happy to report that one Japanese HUDC official made a special trip to Minneapolis to walk across Siah Armajani's bridge connecting Loring Park with the Sculpture Garden.

Sincerely,

Joan Mondale

P.S. Claes Oldenburg and Coosje van Bruggen, of "Spoonbridge and Cherry" fame, were commissioned to create a work for the new Tokyo International Convention Center, or "Big Sight," which is built on a land-fill in Tokyo Bay. "Saw, Sawing" is a giant red-handled handsaw with its blade buried halfway into the ground. Oldenburg described their concept by saying, "The action of cutting through layers represents the process of solving problems which characterizes a convention center." We enjoyed having them for dinner.

November, 1996
What to See in Tokyo

If you are planning to come to Tokyo, the most difficult decision will be choosing what to see.

We suggest visiting the huge Meiji Shrine, a gift to the people from the Meiji emperor (1868-1912). At the Asakusa Shrine, vendors are lined up on both sides of the approaches to the shrine. Nearby is Kappabashi where you can buy all kinds of pots, pans, kitchenware, and plastic food. A quiet visit to the Fukagawa Edo Museum allows you to wander through a reconstructed fishing village of the Edo era (the Tokugawa Shogunate, 1603–1868). Since there are literally hundreds of museums in Tokyo, the

- **We always liked to take our guests to the Meiji Shrine. It was built in honor of the Emperor Meiji, who transformed Japan in the nineteenth century into a modern industrial nation.**

November, 1996 *What to See in Tokyo*

newest and grandest is Tokyo's Museum of Contemporary Art, a showplace of the Tokyo metropolitan government's patronage of the arts. For the most exquisite collection of stoneware pots connected with the tea ceremony, the Hatakeyama Museum is my favorite. And, if you like Warren MacKenzie's straightforward, uncluttered pots, you will enjoy visiting the Mingei-kan, a collection of folk art, textiles, and pottery from the *mingei* tradition (based on Shoji Hamada, Bernard Leach, and Soetsu Yanagi's theories and practice, as found in Mashiko today). Don't forget that all museums charge entrance fees, up to $10 per person.

Should you like to get up early on a Sunday morning, the shrine sales are great for bargain hunters! On the first and last Sundays, Togo Shrine (near the Meiji Shrine) has the biggest sale. On the second and third Sundays, the Hanazono Shrine sale is small but choice. I like to buy vintage kimonos to give as gifts. I take apart the indigo *kasuri* ones from the countryside to make placemats, bedspreads, or patch-

Our son, Ted, and his wife, Pam, visited the Meiji Shrine and were treated to a special dance performance.

work vests. Obis make great table runners and you can wear the sash tied at the upper edge of the obi, the *obiage*, as a scarf. There are lots of blue and white porcelain, antique furniture (including old chests, *tansu*), baskets darkened with age, wooden screens, and all kinds of memorabilia.

There are endless numbers of shops in Tokyo. The three I like the most are The Blue and White in Azabujuban (Amy Kato's single-handed promotion of indigo and white fabrics from rural areas recycled into what Americans would want to buy); Tokyu Hands in Shibuya (you will also need to get there by taxi), where everything imaginable for the home is for sale (I like buying those chops, or stamps, with an ink pad to decorate my letters to friends); and The Oriental Bazaar in Omotesando (as long as you are there, a quick stop at Issey Miyake's fashion showroom is a must).

Kabuki (traditional Japanese theatre) tickets

•
Vivian Mason, Lynda Pederson, and I show off our kimono purchases at a Hanazono Shrine sale.

November, 1996 *What to See in Tokyo*

range from 140 dollars on the main floor to ten dollars in the upper galleries. You can come at 11 a.m. and stay until the last show is over at 9 p.m., eating a picnic supper, *obento*, bought from shops in the lobby. (Be sure to rent the English explanation on tapes.)

Forget about seeing a sumo match. There are just four tournaments a year and tickets for good seats are handed down within families. You can get a pretty good idea of what it is all about by watching the matches on television.

Restaurants range from expensive to more expensive. Dinner can average as much as $250.00 per person. However, for lunch, noodle shops are everywhere and it is perfectly acceptable to put the bowl up to your mouth, shovel the noodles in and slurp while doing so! Kisso,

•
Terumi-san and Fusako-san helped take kimonos apart. Here we are, cutting the seams of a *yukata* to make napkins. I am wearing an indigo dyed kasuri *uwappari* which ties on each side.

LETTERS FROM JAPAN

- Warren and Nancy MacKenzie were invited to lunch by Yoshihiro Takeshita, an antique dealer and old house mover from Kamakura. Peggy Otsuki was a friend of his.

- This is a picture of the main street in Yanaka. We came to know many of the merchants.

November, 1996 *What to See in Tokyo*

in the lower level of the Axis Building in Roppongi, serves a moderately priced Japanese luncheon menu. For dinner, two of the most elegant restaurants we were taken to were Hirumatsu, in Minami-Azabu, and Chez Matsuo, in the old mansion of a successful nineteenth-century merchant. For the hip 30-year-olds, Ninniku-ya ("garlic restaurant") takes no reservations and you must get there early and stand in line. Tableau is decorated with whimsy. Monsoon serves until 4 a.m. And Eleanor Mondale's favorite is Las Chicas. Our newest find is Kiraku in Hiroo. It is a tiny restaurant, designed by an artist, where only one menu is served, chef's choice. (It is not inexpensive!) One of the rooms has blue and white *soba* cups, small bowls for dipping *soba* noodles,

- **Peggy Otsuki was my staff interpreter who was invaluable to me. She is an American, born in Salt Lake City. She accompanied me on my speaking tours, translating, and running the slide machine and the VCR. She knew all the best places to go sight seeing. Kabuki actors were her friends and she was an avid fan of sumo wrestling. She guided our son, William, when he came to visit us.**

lining the walls next to the ceiling. It is connected to Gallery Shun, where Mr. Yuki sells the work of aspiring potters for low prices.

Fritz is always looking for glimpses of old Tokyo as it was before the Great Kanto Plain Earthquake of 1923 and World War II. He discovered the area of tiny shops called Yanaka, near Ueno Park. *Old Tokyo, Walks in the City of the Shogun*, by Sumiko Enbutsu, has a description of this section of Tokyo. A copy of *Tokyo, a Bilingual Atlas*, published by Kodansha, has the vitally necessary map of the subway system.

Be prepared for a tidy, organized, gracious, and polite country where visitors are welcome. *Sumimasen* (excuse me) and *arigato gazaimasu* (thank you) will help you find directions in a country where the old and the new are tightly intertwined.

Sincerely,

Joan Mondale

P.S. My favorite books have been *The Outnation: A Search for the Soul of Japan* by Jonathan Rauch, *36 Views of Mt. Fuji* by Cathy N. Davidson, and *The Secrets of Mariko*, by Elizabeth Bumiller.

December, 1996
Saying Good-Bye and Coming Home

As you may know, Fritz has announced that we are coming home on December 15, 1996. We have been here about three-and-a-half years, the average stay for an ambassador. With newly re-elected governments in both the United States and Japan and major changes in both of those governments, it seemed like a logical time to step down.

We are looking forward to returning, but we are full of many good memories about our stay in Japan. This was the first time we have been "ex-

Prime Minister Hashimoto invited us to his home when we came to say good-bye. He seemed genuinely disappointed when Fritz told him we were leaving Japan.

- To thank Art Zegelbone, our Cultural Affairs officer, who guided my way in the art world, we gave a small dinner party with his closest friends. We presented him with a cake showing Shinjuku i-Land's "Love" sculpture by Robert Indiana. To Fritz's right is Kyoko Mishista, arts program planner for the Tokyo American Center.

- Our last famous guest was Michael Johnson, the Olympic gold metal winner who was the fastest runner in the world. My dress was made from a purple and white, tie-dyed kimono, which I had found at a Hanazono Shrine sale.

pats," living in another country. It has been challenging and we hope these have been good years for the U.S.–Japanese relationship.

We found that saying good-bye in Japan takes more time than saying hello. (It's taken us a full month.) We have made farewell courtesy calls on Their Imperial Majesties, Prime Minister Hashimoto, and other officials of the Japanese government. We have just finished a dizzying round of luncheons, dinners, and receptions to say good-bye to our friends and those with whom we have worked.

This has been a "toothpick farewell." When we visited the prime minister, Mrs. Hashimoto whispered in my ear that the tiny pot I made which I had given to her now held toothpicks on their dining room table. And when the former foreign minister, Yohei Kono, came to our residence with his 33-year-old son Taro, who had just been elected to the Diet, he brought a wooden box with a bird perched on top, which contained toothpicks. By pushing a knob down, the lid opens and the bird pops up with a toothpick in its beak. An identical box sits on his diningroom table.

It was interesting talking to young Taro about campaigning. His mother has made so many friends seeking votes for her husband, that Taro thought it best if his father spent all his time in his *own* district, campaigning for his *own* re-election.

We leave with much admiration and appreciation for our foreign service officers and with renewed respect for the quality of our military leadership. Sally Tobin, whose husband Rear

Admiral Byron Tobin is commander of the U.S. Naval Forces in Japan, told me that they have been married for 29 years and she has moved 29 times.

We shall always remember the warmth and kindness of the Japanese people, so many of whom have been educated in the United States, who have lived among us, or have traveled throughout our country. They are filled with admiration for the freedom with which we conduct our lives and for all the choices which are open to each one of us.

I particularly want to thank the *Hill & Lake Press* for inviting me to make my reports to its readers.

- **One of the last sights we saw as we drove down the long driveway, past the garden, was the smiling face of a guard saying *"sayonara"* and thank you as he closed the gates behind us.**

December, 1996 *Saying Good-Bye and Coming Home*

Above all, Fritz and I are happy to be coming home to be with our family and friends again. When Fritz called our six-year-old grandson Louie to tell him that we were coming home, Louie said, "I think you made a good decision. Now can you come to my hockey games?" The answer was "yes," with a big smile!

Sincerely,

Joan Mondale

P.S. We were filled with anticipation after the eleven hour, non-stop Northwest flight from Tokyo. Looking out of the plane's windows, we saw the ground covered with snow and we knew it would be cold. When we left Tokyo, it was 70° above zero. When we landed, it was 20° below, but we were instantly warmed by the sight of Ted and Pam and the grandchildren with William, our younger son. (Eleanor would join us later from Los Angeles for Christmas.) We loved Japan, but it was wonderful to be home again.

Louie came to greet us at the Minneapolis airport with his newly-won ice hockey trophy
Photo by Chris Polydoroff, St. Paul Pioneer Press.

LETTERS FROM JAPAN

- Fritz held an impromptu press conference with the reporters who met us at the airport. Berit wanted to hear what was going on, so she stood, wearing her leopard patterned coat, next to her grandfather to listen in.

Photo by Chris Polydoroff, St. Paul Pioneer Press

- One of the times I looked forward to the most was reading bedtime stories to Amanda.

March, 1997
From Ambassador to Grandpa

We are so happy to be home again, surrounded by family and friends. We're peppered with many questions. One we are always asked is "How did you like Japan?" We had an incredible adventure, living in that complex and ancient culture. Both Fritz and I are very grateful to have had the opportunity to serve in that remarkable country. We made many friends and we feel greatly enriched by our experiences there. We shall always cherish those years.

One is struck by the anomaly of the outward modernity of Japan on the one hand: huge office buildings, fashionable clothing, high-tech industries, and a democratic form of government. On the other hand, we've been impressed with the resilience and strength of their very different and unique Japanese culture, with

Pam and Ted with Berit, Amanda, and Louie Mondale, Christmas, 1996.

roots and traditions that are many centuries old.

Everyone wants to know about Crown Princess Masako, the Harvard graduate who, after a six-year courtship, left her career in the Japanese foreign service to marry the crown prince. She will likely one day become Japan's empress. By her marriage, she became a member of the Imperial family, governed by centuries of tradition and guided by the Imperial Household Agency. She has assumed the role of a supportive wife. Her life is secluded and protected. Only recently has she spoken at public events without her husband. The Japanese people are fascinated with her and wonder what her role will be, should she become empress in the future. Her mother-in-law, the current empress, broke tradition by insisting on raising the crown prince, his brother, and his sister herself, instead of handing them over to a nanny. She even went so far as to make their *obento* school lunches every day.

I am often asked about the role of women in Japan and the question is whether Japanese women will change their expected roles of fulfilling the commonly-held concept that a woman's place is only in the home.

Many wives seen quite satisfied to stay at home, where volunteer work is not as widespread as in the U.S. and babysitters are frowned upon. They become "education mothers," focusing their energies on getting their children into the right schools, colleges, and universities. A diploma from a top-rated school is a guarantee of a good job lasting for a lifetime. Other women seek to continue their careers after

March, 1997 *From Ambassador to Grandpa*

marriage, albeit with difficulty.

Perhaps because I worked so closely with the Japanese arts community, I am often asked my appraisal of the art scene there. The Japanese have a very impressive aesthetic instinct. There is hardly a day when a major orchestra isn't playing, a dance group perforrming, Kabuki and Noh theater giving shows, or an exhibition of visual arts in one of the many museums devoted to contemporary art, both Japanese and American. The quality, range of interest, and support given to the arts is very strong.

Being a potter, I was taken by their love of clay. Many a man's face softened as we talked about our favorite potters and the kilns I had visited. Invariably I was told that there was always just one more potter I should meet.

I was also very encouraged by their growing interest in supporting art in public places. Currently inere are plans to have art installed in the new subway stop, Tameike-sanno, near the U.S. Embassy in Tokyo.

Sincerely,

Joan Mondale

- **The sticker Amy Katoh uses in her shop to wrap purchases: "Otafuku", good fortune.**

147